We Tell You Our Stories
From The Afterlife
Direct Messages *From* The Other Side
Via
Full body Open Deep Trance Channel and Medium
April Crawford

Title: **We Tell You Our Stories From The Afterlife: Direct Messages From The Other Side**

Authors: April Crawford, Seventy-Five Individuals

Publisher: Connecting Wave
2629 Foothill Blvd.
Unit # 353
La Crescenta, CA 91214
www.ConnectingWave.com

ISBN: 978-1-7367020-1-7

Book Design & Introduction: Allen Crawford

For Author Information:
www.AprilCrawford.com

For Free "Inner Whispers" Newsletters:
www.InnerWhispers.net

Other books via April Crawford:
www.AprilCrawfordBooks.com

Podcasts: www.TheInnerWhispersInterviews.com

For Permissions: Publisher@ConnectingWave.com

INTRODUCTION

The messages in this book are all in the form of letters written from the other side by those telling their stories. These messages are **not** what is commonly referred to as the result of "automatic writing" or "relay mediumship".

Each of the writers was given one writing session to come through fully themselves via a true Full Body Open Deep Trance Channel named April Crawford. To be clear, the primary activities of April Crawford in this field are to allow various nonphysical beings of all types and levels to speak, walk around the room, have a glass of wine if they want, have some goat cheese if they want, and to look whomever they are speaking with in the eye and use full body language, which they all do.

The written messages in this book came about as a secondary benefit of the twice weekly writing of the "Inner Whispers" newsletters and various books by the nonphysical Causal Plane Entity and guide that we named VERONICA (because "she" would not give us a label when she first came through more than thirty years ago).

Other than this introduction's mention, VERONICA did not take part in this book other than perhaps facilitating some of the writers. This is amazing in that VERONICA handles virtually all of the consultations/readings with clients and has done so for decades, talking with thousands of clients worldwide, plus literally thousands of in-person private sessions with me. Oh yes, and VERONICA has written most of the books….. so far.

All of these messages have been written in first, final, and only draft. In fact, the writers could not edit them even if they wanted to, as they only had one continuous opening. Many others wanted to and still do want to write their messages, and as mentioned, this is not our main or even secondary activity in this field.

Probably all of the writers could have spoken and walked around the room if they wanted to, but that was not the opportunity afforded them. It was piggy backing on the writing of the newsletters and books by VERONICA that gave them this one-shot opportunity to say whatever they wanted to. And it was a rare shot indeed when you think that there are 75 messages here while billions of people have "died" and many of them would probably have loved to get a spot in line. (Note that there are still more messages of this type coming through at least a few times each month.) Still, we do what time allows given everything else and the considerable time seven days a week, every week, that April Crawford dedicates to allow clients to speak directly with VERONICA. Plus we do weekly Podcasts and the twice weekly all original content "Inner Whispers" Newsletters (which are free at www.InnerWhispers.net).

Now the fact that I tend to be somewhat of a purest when it comes to very limited editing of third party material like this will cause some issues for what I call strict "red pen types". In order to preserve the integrity of each individual's message (and the process under which it occurred) to the greatest extent possible, the letters are presented almost exactly as written by them using April Crawford's physical form to do so. This means various levels of grammar, spelling, and writing ability from individual to individual are apparent. Plus the time constraints that they needed to deal with given only single session to write and their inability to edit their own writing came into play here. So, if the less than perfect grammar or punctuation bothers some readers, think of what it would be like in an audio book or if the writers were speaking instead of writing. They took their one opportunity under such very rare, and for most of them, challenging circumstances. After all, they are writing from their afterlife. Think of what it would mean to you to get such a message from one of your loved ones or friends. Then think of what it would be like for them to communicate in any way with the physical existence they recently crossed out of. It is unlikely that you, or they, would quibble about the grammar or punctuation.

A Personal Note: If the "red pen" comments above come across as defensive to some, they are. In 30 years of doing this type of work and at this level, it has constantly amazed me that some people tend to point out things that compared to the magnitude of these types of communications seem to be absolutely trivial in nature. I call it "missing the forest for the trees." Again, just a personal note.

Having said the above, there have been a few instances where a comma or two have been added to make the reading easier. The same goes for apostrophes as the writers almost never used them. Also sentences that grammatically would be considered questions, were often expressed as statements or stream of consciousness thoughts. In those cases the writers ended sentences with periods rather than question marks. They also seemed not to use contractions which have mostly been left as two words as originally written. Hopefully the content and their personal stories will be compelling enough to overlook grammar or spelling issues. Also, I chose all of the message headings. The headings are all quotes from the individual letters. as none of the actual writers used headings or titles. The exception to this is the title "A Note From Mom".

Most of the writers started off their letters with "Dear Friend" as a convention, or perhaps it was just a way to start the writing flowing for some. Most wrote in long hand although some printed their messages. Some were far more articulate than others. All relayed heart felt very personal accounts and messages that they felt were important to share.

~ Allen, Facilitator for April Crawford

CONTENTS

Message	Number

Message	Number

Message Number

1

I Never Liked Airplanes

Dear friend,

I never liked airplanes. They were an invitation to doom as far as I was concerned. I never got on one until I was older. It was still a disaster any way you looked at it. Since my children had chosen to scatter to various parts of the country, I was left with no choice if I wanted to see them. So there I was twice a year getting in a vehicle that I was sure wasn't going to get me there in one piece.

Everyone hated Christmas travel, but I sort of liked all the people beside me in my terror. There was comfort in the masses I always used to say. Everyone was paying more attention I thought. I was wrong, but then again it wasn't quite Christmas either. It was just a crowded plane. I was wedged between a wailing child and an obnoxious drinker who kept heckling the flight attendant for another vodka. I wanted to tell him that he should just shut up, but after three drinks he was slumped over in his seat for what I hoped was the remainder of the flight.

The wailing child fell into a restless sleep only bothering his exhausted mother for a moment after takeoff. I stretched my feet as forward as I could but kept my hands clenched to the arms of my seat. Thus I began my vigil until we were safely on the ground again.

My eyes grew heavy midway through the flight and I found myself dreaming of times gone by. After all, at sixty-five one has quite a few experiences to draw upon in the dream state. I readily submitted knowing that being unconscious was the best way to speed up time. Hopefully upon awakening I would be at my destination.

Sleep overtook me and I would have stayed that way if the plane had not jolted suddenly to the right. It snapped me out of my unconscious state into the harsh reality of foul weather in the air. At least that was my first thought. Unfortunately it wasn't my last thought. The plane began a downward spiral for what reason I was not sure.

The air became thin and I grappled with everyone else for my oxygen mask. I found myself wishing I had been more attentive during the safety lectures at the beginning of the flight. What had they said anyway? When the mask fell down I pulled it to my face. I felt a lot better and was able to assess the rest of the cabin.

Most of the passengers were unconscious. The screaming baby was silent, wrapped in his mother's arms as she cried. The drinker next to me never regained consciousness. He was lost in a hell of alcohol unaware he was suffocating. I tried to attach his mask but the angle of the plane threw me in a different position. I was unable to reach him.

There was now pandemonium everywhere. The attendants were attempting to calm passengers, but most were feeble in their effort. They were just as scared as the rest of us.

I looked around in a surreal calmness. Out of most of the people I should have been the most panicked, but I wasn't. I knew we were in trouble, but oddly felt fine with it. The momentum of the downward spiral accelerated. The cries of the others diminished. Were we really going to crash? Yes, we were. It was a fact as I clung to my seat hoping for a reprieve. The worst of my fears realized in the next moments. I decided to close my eyes while waiting for the inevitable. Why was I so calm? I was going to die in the way I feared most. Was it unfair or just a result?

My oxygen mask failed while we were still plummeting. Everyone around me now was silent. Were they already dead? Why oh why was I still conscious? I did not wish to remain until the end. Why couldn't God be merciful and allow me to slip quietly out of my body?

When it occurred to me that this was not probable, I started to think of heaven. Since it was so close, why not will myself out of body?

I saw a bright light to my right as we approached the ground. It was luminous and inviting. It caught my attention so fully that I forgot that we were going down. In fact, so provocative was the energy that I felt compelled to move towards it. I unbuckled my seatbelt, which was no easy feat in a nose dive. I stood facing the light. The wailing child also stood next to me silent and focused. I whispered "let's go" while we held hands moving towards it. It must be the gates of heaven I thought. Well whatever it was, it was better than exploding to smithereens on an unforgiving ground that was rapidly approaching.

The child and I took a flying leap into the light. There was no sound. The air was still while I sensed a presence of others, but knew they were not from the recently departed plane. This was new territory with new characters. Was it heaven?

I don't think so.

Was it an afterlife?

Obviously.

What was I going to do with it?

Live it.

Whatever it was.

I could feel the child beside me, knowing it was appropriate to take it along the path. Behind me was a plane crash, before me was opportunity.

I chose to walk towards it.

I still don't like airplanes.

I plan on manifestation within a time frame without them.

I am waiting for my children to arrive before I move on, as they are still connected to me.

The plane no longer exists in the time line, but I exist eternally. I survived my worst fear. That has to account for something.

****

2

The Gain of Experience

Dear Friend,

When I face the path I come from I see the turmoil of my surroundings. The warmth of my mother's breast would not still my cries. I felt her weep when I would not suckle, but there was no milk to quench my thirst. Parched, I turned away knowing that my thirst was not to be satisfied in this life. It was only a brief thought, but telling for my mind to recall.

I remember the dust as she struggled to shield my face. My nostrils filled anyway, drying them until they bled. My lips moistened by a cloth, I lick them until they are chaffed. I hear the scraping of pounded sorghum in a bowl. The other children reach their fingers in but I have not the strength.

A pain comes in my belly while I cry for my mother to come stop it. Is that not the way of mothers? Are they not inclined to save their children?

I look around the place of my family, feeling despair. The ways of this culture, not what I expected. I am hungry. Sores multiply upon the skin erupting daily until I wish of another time and place. The knaw in my belly grows larger. I am but several months before the one year, yet I know of the lack quite well. Even the hand of my mother cannot separate me from the ache of hunger.

She weeps at my misfortune, knowing her hand in it all.

We understand mutually that there is no place meant for the despair and anger, other than I feel my flesh burn with heat as it slides from the correct place on my arms. Woe to the children I hear echo in my head. How did I arrive at such a place? The choice to continue hovers above me. Should I? The curve of my mother's arm comforts me. At least I am not without love.

I remember resting upon her hip shielded by a cloth that wrapped over her shoulder. My breath came in short movements followed by a pain in the chest. It seems that all of me is ablaze with a foreign substance that is inclined to murder me while I sleep.

There appears a man who feels helpful. He places objects through my skin to "hydrate", so he says. I cry for my mother who waits anxiously away from me. It is disturbing to be away from her grasp. I recognize that the wish is to help, but my mother needs my strength to survive my death.

The word death comes to me like a lullaby while I drift between the choices. I am young. So very young for such a rough experience, but I cling to life for clarity. Why did I do this? The answers leave me desperate to draw a conclusion. Any conclusion.

I nestle into her arms. Again my belly still an echo of hunger that pounds loudly in my bloodstream. The pain needs a resolution, but can I leave the breast of a mother who loves me? Will her heart harden with bitterness if I depart? I cannot know. The only knowing is the discomfort, so I make the decision based on a physical reaction.

My eyes close.

The breath stops. I hear the laments of my mother, but there is nothing to be done for her sorrow. It will occur again until she is hardened to the casualties of her life.

I drift away from that tortured form….. realizing for the first time….. why? The appreciation of the environment surprising, since it was so physically debilitating. The gain of experience was the why. The idea confusing, but as I continue to drift away I take the lack with me to be thought of again later. It will give perspective to another time and place.

****

3

Oddly, It Didn't Hurt

Dear friend,

I always faint at the sight of blood. Childhood mishaps that left my knees ripped of flesh were always much worse than a bruised shin. My parents used to tease me that I would never succeed in a medical profession. I would be a quivering lump on the floor at the first glance of blood.

So throughout my life the avoidance was always clear. No Blood…..thank you. I became a school teacher right out of college. There had been an opening at a private school for a little less money but it was close to home. I could literally walk to work. The children were a blessing. They filled my days with their inquisitive minds and zeal for life. Third grade was the absolute best age. I hoped I could teach the level indefinitely.

There were a few playground accidents that caused a bit of a problem because it meant I participated with all the skinned elbows and knees. I actually was pretty proud of myself. The chill in my bones was becoming fairly controllable. That is if the bleeding was at a minimum. A young 1st grade boy slashed himself on a nail once that pretty much did me in. Little Joey needed fifteen stitches to sew up his arm. I needed about fifteen sips of wine to calm down. We both, however, got through it.

It was a crisp fall morning that I decided to walk to school. I had left my brief case at home because today I was treating my class to a movie and pizza in the afternoon. It was a reward for doing well on a spelling test that was well deserved.

The air had that bit of frost that signals the coming of winter. I inhaled the cold air feeling pretty damn lucky to be alive. A gust of wind sent some fallen leaves swirling about me. So I pulled my sweater tighter across my shoulders. I glanced down for a brief second as I stepped down off the curb into the street. The school was right in front of me. Some of my students were already on the front steps waiting for me.

In that moment there was a loud roar that caused my head to jerk up. I found myself looking into the eyes of a sports car filled with teenage boys. All I can recall is their wide eyes of terror as they slammed into me at full speed. Oddly it didn't hurt. The feeling of flotation filled me as I saw the school flip acrobatically away from me. I heard screaming from somewhere. Perhaps it was coming from my own throat.

Suddenly I was on the ground but the arrival there was lost to me. There was a familiar smell that immediately turned my stomach….. it was blood.

There were a lot of people hovering over me. Each one kept talking, hoping to keep me from slipping away. A siren cried in the distance, but I didn't feel hurt. In fact there was not feeling at all. Just a lot of blood. Surprisingly that was not a problem either. The surreal play of events looked like a scene from a nickelodeon. Feelings of detachment filled me as I began to notice other scenes. None of them resembled the school or my neighborhood. All of them bustled with activity that had nothing to do with the accident that surrounded me.

The voices calling me back became distant while other whispers became more predominant. It was a reminder of how color changes with water paints. Two or three separate colors blending together to form a new color. So preoccupied was I with that, that the blood was no longer an issue, neither was the idea of movement away from the scene.

My eyes focused on the other place and suddenly I was there. Thought of separation from those who loved me, however, I knew it wasn't forever. They would soon follow in reunion. So I left the street where the body lay and moved to a new place of existence.

I am at peace.

****

4

I Am Only A Breath Away

Dear Friend,

The floor feels cool upon my cheek although I am afraid to open my eyes. Within my mind the body remains whole, not damaged in an unforgivable way. Outside the prognosis is bleak if I open my eyes. The hope of time suspended diminishes as I lay there. Thoughts of who will find me race through my mind as I move forward towards a glimmer of light not far from my grasp. I should be more upset. The idea of learning so soon not occurring to me….. at least not recently.

What happened to me?

The sharp pain in my head dismissed as a headache, knocking me to the floor with its violent burst. It didn't hurt for long, making me think that it would pass with all being well again. So startling was the impact that I failed to notice I had also stopped breathing.

The floor still cool upon my cheek, the focus now above me. I reach up to touch it hoping it will lead me to somewhere else. The view before me becomes intermingled so that I am uncertain which is real. Laughing to myself, the realization that it doesn't matter occurs to me.

My cheek no longer embraces the floor. My mind focused now on the other things as the glimmer unfolds to a destination. The more I think about it, the more it expands into comfort. Wherever it is, I feel destined to follow it. The thought of what I leave behind dulls as the connection grows stronger. It will all be fine I tell myself. They will find me….. yes, but not in crisis, only peace.

So I move ever forward, the pain subsiding into a distant memory.

Feel not pity for me as the path is comforting in your absence. We will cross ways again. Of that I am sure.

Feel me in your quiet moments, as I am only a breath away. Just a breath, that is all.

****

5

Never Lost

Dear Friend,

I stand on the cliff that overlooks the home we have created. So many times we have sat here together contemplating the progress of our dream. It is in this spot that what we share came into existence. On our first arrival there was nothing there. It was through our thought and conversation that the house was built. So many pitfalls while it progressed to the cozy cottage it is today. Each addition rising with our laughter and love. From this point of view I see it all with such clarity.

I shield my eyes from the sun. The roof of the barn reflects it. We never thought it would be a problem. It only meant that we would wait until the beams of light began to fade into the twilight. The night sky equally beautiful as the lights began to emerge from the house. We made sure that the twinkle of lights from the city was far enough away not to diminish the natural glow of planets and stars. How many nights did we hold hands crouched together upon the gravel?

All of the thoughts of our marriage flow and ebb through me with such energy. If I choose I can go into each of them. Not to relive them but to caress their intricate pulse as they continue into infinity.

The starry sky fills me, prompting a decision to make a night of it. I unfold the blanket, stretching it so I can pull the ends over my feet. Remember how we used to fight over blanket rights? It always ended in giggles with neither of us on the blanket at all. Those are the treasures I think about from our cliff. They crescendo within me. I reach out to touch your hand. It grasps me lightly. I feel your presence as it warms me from the night air. It's just like it was from those many times. You and I together as one, creating a path filled with memories. They will always be dear to my heart.

Never forgotten.

Never lost.

Always within.

So even though my grip on your hand may loosen, it doesn't indicate that I'm gone. I'm merely waiting for you on our cliff. My body no longer a viable means of communication, we will resort to the memories.

Sit out on our cliff.

I'll be there.

Kiss me once then move away for I am no longer in residence. My spirit flows with you. Our life together a testament to our experience in many existences. We will always meet at the cliff.

We've done it before.

I simply remind you.

****

6

It Was Me

Dear Friend,

I was afraid, so very afraid. I always thought I would live forever. Never did I consider that I would stop living so quickly. The idea of having thirty more years was at least a comfort to me.

In my general health it never occurred to me that I might have a flaw. My body had always felt strong. Other people would be envious, I thought, of my good fortune to be in such great shape.

I still recall the day it happened. Up for my early morning jog I had bent over to tie my shoelaces. The nauseous feeling hit me hard. It wasn't like me to have these experiences. After I stood up it continued. Perhaps I should have done something about it right then and there, but I didn't.

My stomach felt out of sorts continually throughout the day. Several of my colleagues were actually pleased that I felt bad. "Just kidding", they said with a wink. They thought it was a case of the flu. Much to my chagrin I thought so as well.

It wasn't till I came home from work that an intense pang hit me.

I felt as if someone had reached inside my chest cavity to

squeeze my heart. Falling to my knees the struggle to maintain consciousness overwhelmed me.

Who should I call?

Could I call by myself?

Where was my cell phone?

I could feel another attack preparing itself inside of me. In this moment the fear of the unknown filled me. Would the next jolt finish me off?

I didn't know…..

I just didn't know.

When it hit I remember feeling violent pain. The back of my head hit the linoleum with a whack. Stars flashed before my eyes but still I did not lose consciousness. I kinda wished I had. The fear was gripping me so violently that I was at a loss for a game plan.

Was I going to die?

Would it continue to be this painful?

I wanted to cry out to God or anyone who could spare me. It was not to be. The pain continued and I was afraid.

So very afraid.

My body had betrayed me in every sense. I did not want to die but it was evident that I was down to my fingertips and toes. So focused in the fear I didn't notice anything else.

The pain and fear encompassing my every thought. If this is what it's like to die, it is indeed a painful experience. Why couldn't it just by over?

I found myself on the floor, stillness pulsing through me. My breath shallow practically nonexistent. I could not feel my heart. It was silent. Yet I was conscious. I should have felt exhaustion, but I felt fine. I should have called for help but I didn't feel like I needed to.

There was a knock at the door. I should have been unable to answer it. Yet there I stood with my hand on the handle. Who would be arriving now that it was too late?

It never dawned on me that after all of it I was still there. I felt lighter. I felt many things but what I wasn't prepared for was the sight at the door.

It was me.

****

7

Yes. We All Had Died. But Somehow We all Still Exist

Dear Friend,

A drip of sweat trickled slowly down the middle of my shoulder blades. It's descent irritating me in my attempt to relax. I would have been better if the incessant heat had not envelope me so tightly. It would have been better with a breeze. A small inhale of breath for the heaviness in the air. It gave off a feeling of confinement with no release. The whole experience heightened by that small drop of sweat. I might have survived if it had not been for that. At least that is what I consoled myself within the final moments.

You really need a sense of comfort then, at least I did. A speech of encouragement coming you believe from God. However if there was a God, why would he allow such foolish choices that resulted in this kind of predicament? It angered me in the end round.

I should have been in another place this afternoon. The plan had not included a plane ride. Alas though, there I was on the way to a meeting rescheduled abruptly in Washington. The smartest and the safest route was by train, so I was told. The claim that it would be an equal amount of travel time still ringing in my ears as I sit buried under tons of steel. I should have listened to my initial reaction of how dumb an idea it was.

The twisting of metal is an interesting sound, like something out of Star Wars. It took me a full minute to discern what was occurring. By then of course it was too late to do anything. If one could reverse time I might have been able to avoid this predicament.

Oddly enough it was painless. One of my arms was invisible under the shredded seat next to me. I recall wondering where it was, though not with alarm.

I could not figure out which way was up. It seemed like I was upside down but it was difficult to figure out. A man whose name I did not know sat doubled over next to me. He made no sound. In fact the only sound was a hiss of steam and an occasional drip of liquid. There was no way of knowing where it came from. Thinking was becoming a chore from which I desperately wanted to escape.

I was able to lean my head back for relief. The warmness of the train car becoming oppressive. Trying not to focus on it I knew time was limited. I shut my eyes to rest. I did not feel like I needed to escape. I could not have even if I wanted to. My breath becoming more shallow with thoughts, unfolding memories before me. I became one with them.

I think that's when it actually happened, the passing I mean. Scenes from my life became available for participation and I just went there.

It did not occur to me to return to the train. I just kept going. The bead of sweat between my shoulder fell to the ground mixing with the blood of the others. Yes. We all had died, but somehow we all still exist.

I move forward with the promise of more experience. The rest of the expected life taken from me to be fulfilled in another. I should have felt robbed, but I do not.

Life begins and ends for various reasons. My choices leading the way my body follows the path. My soul released to continue the journey to expansion.

****

8

As I Passed Through The Body, I Found The Release Incredible

Dear Friend,

It has been said that death stalks all of us and that no one escapes. A grim experience awaits those who do not live within the light of God. Such a tale has haunted the hearts of man for generations. My finite moment of the life cycle does indeed await us all. It fills the pattern of our lives driving us through choices that might have been made differently if they were truly known.

I reach into the depths of my psyche only to find the wrath of linear stealing the opportunity to get the lesson. The design of multiple existence the only ideal way to find redemption. The struggle to believe always difficult for me. I could taste the bitter sweet brew of deceit as I rested upon my hospice bed. The unfairness of my one shot reverberating in my heart as I felt the heat of my blood go cold. The panic in the realization that it's out of control seizes you in its grip, leaving nothing to salvage.

I recall the fables of my youth told to me by the sisters of faith. "Praise God and be righteous," they whispered during my childhood. "Live well on fear of the God who created you." By doing so the creation left me unable to navigate properly through my parallel existences.

As I lay on the sheet awaiting the moment, it occurs to me that God really had nothing to do with the current circumstance. It was what others told me, that I believed as truth. However there was always inner knowing, which because I didn't trust myself enough, I didn't embrace.

There was no disappointment in my heart. Actually it was a relief to be free of the constraints of what had been created. As I passed through the body, I found the release incredible. It felt like the shedding of a fifty-pound weight. The remarkable encounter with myself left me breathless for more.

I know I must return to the body to complete the cycle of this lesson, but the desire for more accuracy in creation dwells heavily upon me. I await another opportunity to complete what I set out to do.

Death is not grim. It's merely a function of physical existence.

****

9

A Note From Mom

I always knew what a gift you were. From the first time I looked at your little scrunched face I was hopelessly in love. It was always my intention to see you through to adulthood. You were my future, my hopes, and my dreams.

When I became ill the idea of death seemed remote since I still felt fine. We played everyday while the disease began to disassemble my body. Silently it spread until my days consisted mainly of trying to just sit up. I could see you too in the distance while I tried to have a moment of peace. The struggle almost too much to endure.

I want you to know that I wanted to stay. The fear of separating from you making the transition difficult.

That last day your eyes beckoning me to play yet understanding that I could barely move. My body beginning to shut down while fighting the best that I could.

The denial crept through me as I resolved to play with you more tomorrow. If I could just rest a bit I would feel better.

There was a release inside me when the sun went down. A brief moment where I realized the sun would come up without me tomorrow.

As I closed my eyes it was merely to concentrate upon not feeling nauseated. My mind began to examine the last moments of my life. It was like I was really in them feeling the experience all over again. One of the best of course was finding out I was pregnant with you.

In these places I was aware of people moving about me. They all seemed so unimportant while I was with you. It was like a dream and these moments the true reality.

It was the breathing that proved most difficult. I wanted to open my eyes because there was a feeling of being transported. It was most likely the hospital but there was no way to be sure.

The numbness of the medication began to dissipate making me feel stronger. Whatever was in the IV was working.

I could feel a new energy come into me as the nausea left. I sat up with unexpected ease to see everyone looking anxiously upon me. They had not brought you along, which was a shame because there was a feeling of wellness. I think I could've actually played blocks on the floor with you.

It was confusing when no one acknowledged I was now able to sit up, or anything else. I went from one person to the next attempting to get through to them. No one even looked at me, so focused they were upon the bed. There were even a few tears, which seemed ridiculous. This was a joyous occasion.

I went for the door hoping that someone maybe had brought you along. If you were waiting outside I just couldn't wait to hold you.

As I turned back it was curious to see all of them clustered around the bed. What were they looking at? I managed to look between the bodies to a strange sight. There I was quietly resting. How could that be? Here I was awake and healthy. Was I dreaming?

A hand touched my shoulder and turned me towards it. Oh my God! It was my mother, more beautiful than I remembered.

"What are you doing here?" I asked.

The feelings inside were bursting with emotion. I just wanted to hug her tightly. It had been a long time since I had seen her.

"It's time," she said.

"Time?"

"Time for what?"

All of the information swirling about me, I turned back to myself on the bed. The reality now coming forward. I had lost the battle.

"What about Cody?" I said, my eyes filling with tears. My only thoughts now are with you my dear boy.

My mother, your grandmother explained it all. We will both be by your side whenever you need us. We are not gone, only transcended to a different form. It's sort of like your super heroes you love so much.

I am free of the pain that hindered my ability to stay. I am free.

Remember playing on the floor in the living room. We can whenever we want to.

I wrote to tell you that it is important for you to know that nothing ever ends or dies. We just evolve. Some get there sooner than others.

I love you.

Mom

****

10

Now I Can Tell You It Was All True. All Of It.

Dear Friend,

I miss you. Not that I am far but the lack of physical connection leaves me a bit undone. The weariness of my old form took a toll upon our relationship, that is for sure. Once we had all the facts there was a certain optimism that I might have a chance to beat it. Too bad we couldn't do a virtual tour of my insides. Then we could have known the complete truth and prepared a bit better.

The cancer started in my stomach progressing rapidly until the chemo. A restful period which was hopeful followed by a tumor in my brain. Shrinking it was easy. We joked that a few brain cells probably got diminished as well. I could have done without the brain cells actually, if there had been more time with you.

Thank you for sitting with me in those final days. It did not look like I was paying attention, but I was.

The medication drew so much energy out of me. Just breathing was difficult. The touch of your hand guided me. Without it the sense of loss would have been too overwhelming. I did not want to die. Clinging desperately I fought until I could not anymore. The fear of nothingness and the realization it was over terrifying. Not sure if I believed all the religious stuff, wanting to but afraid that it just might be a big lie. My faith not as strong as the cancer.

Now I can tell you it was all true. All of it.

It goes way beyond what we were told. To die is not the end. Again, my only difficulty is that we are vibrating at a different frequency. Thus we are unable to touch the way we used to. I miss that so much, so I bide my time until you are with me. If you can pay attention to the little things. There are moments when I can actually move physical and touch things. It takes a lot of concentration, but is possible. Know in your heart of hearts whether you see anything or not, and that I am right with you.

Always.

Keep this note with your as a promise of that.

I miss you.

Soon that will change and we will be together forever.

Me.

****

11

Close Your Eyes….. Feel Me

Dear Friend,

At first there was sadness. It was the goodbye part that filled me with much emptiness. Your eyes filled with tears, your hand squeezing mine. I really tried to respond but it seemed there was nothing left for me energy wise. Despair that this was happening along with anger. Helpless physical. Helpless on my path to spirit. The unknown spread before me in an endless path. I wished for my Ma, she was such a religious woman. If she had been at my side she would have reminded me of all the Sunday school lessons that would have helped in the moment.

Alas, she was already where I was going. So far there was no inkling that she would be there to meet me. The sadness was overwhelming so that closing my eyes was scary. I wanted to keep your face in my sight as long as I could. I wanted to say "Don't cry", but I couldn't. I wanted to squeeze your hand as well, but I did not have the strength….. so sad.

I watched your tears well up and overflow down your cheeks. The steady drips on the sheet counting the moments I had left. My eyes follow one droplet to your hands for beside it were another pair of hands.

At first I thought they were a nurse's, but it dawned on me that I recognized them. In a last burst of strength I looked up to see who they belonged to. The eyes that looked back at me were not crying, in fact they were twinkling. It was Ma.

I wanted to tell her immediately all the things we had been through. How scared I was of dying, how I missed her. She placed her hands upon my cheeks. She said not to be afraid of death, it was already occurring. I turned my head back to you, but the vision was already diminished. Panicked, I turned back to Ma.

"What should I do?"

Ma smiled at me the same way she used to when I was a kid. The fear subsided but the sadness remained. How could I exist anywhere without you? The thought leaving me in despair.

Ma as usual showed me the way, just as she did in life. I realized that I can be with you in spirit while you are still physical. The prospect lighting up my whole being. I now constantly search for ways to let you know I am right at your side, forever.

Close your eyes….. feel me.

I do my best at setting out signs of my presence. I will be the first you see when you come here.

The time for that will come.

Do not miss me. My energy is very happy to hold you close.

You are not alone.

Just a while longer my love.

****

12

The Blow To My Head Came Swiftly

Dear Friend,

The blow to my head came swiftly. The sound of it reverberating in my ears long after impact. I want to say it hurt like hell because on some levels it did. The full reality of it included a buzzing that not only left me dizzy, but nauseous as well.

My eyes lost their focus as the darkness came like a window blind slowly cutting my vision until there was no more. The pounding of blood through my neck seemed to magnify with every heartbeat. The realization of what had occurred sending panic ridden messages to my brain.

I felt the collapse of my body to the ground. Amazing how hard the ground is when you fall abruptly upon it. My arms waving wildly in an attempt to break the fall. My head hitting itself again upon impact reigniting the pain.

Sweet relief as I became unconscious. Maybe a deep sleep would allow me to feel better upon rising. Images pass through my thoughts creating dreams of intrigue. Each scenario one where I was attempting to overcome an obstacle. The solution just out of my reach while running down an endless corridor in the attempt.

I remember awakening briefly in what appeared to be a

hospital. There were individuals who leaned over me asking questions. I could barely make out the words, so painful it was to think. My vision so blurred their outlines not recognizable. All I wanted to do was to return to my dream state. My head too heavy to lift, it also felt like my brain had turned to mush.

And the pain, the pain undeniably the worst I had ever felt.

Would it go away?

I tried to remember what happened but I couldn't. There was no one who would mourn my death. All of my loved ones had already crossed over long ago. It was just myself left in the world. The pain stayed as I began to wonder if it was worth the struggle. I heard the word "coma" mentioned by those who attended me. Somewhere in my thoughts I remembered that comas could last a very long time. So I made a decision to just go.

Go to where? I was not certain, but I wanted to be free of the pain that was occurring. I went down the corridor of my mind searching for the way. It came without warning just like the blow to my head. Releasing my grip on what I thought was me, I realized how much more there was. My head ceased throbbing. My vision cleared. I felt better.

The vision of myself in a sterile bed hooked up to many machines came into view. The injury was ghastly. The bandages making me look deformed and old. Surely there was no escape from this physically. I would not recover, but that was okay with me. I suddenly had the clarity of other possibilities. Walking down the corridor I began to encounter my parents, my siblings, and yes, a lost love or two. My reunion joyous, a party so-to-speak.

Never has there been regret in my decision. I am with those I love….. the possibilities endless.

****

13

What Did Greet Me

Dear friend,

You may not have considered the moment of death yet in your life. It lurks outside waiting for an opportunity to descend upon your consciousness. Death is synonymous with the finite or the end. The light extinguished with a breath never to inhale the fragrance of the day again.

All rather morbid considering that death is none of that. From my perspective it was actually a release from a personal creation that I wished to run from. Little did I know the issues stay with you, only to rear their ugly heads at another point in time.

I spent the last moment of this past life fearing death rather than understanding that it's simply a passage. The continuance of my consciousness was not a consideration.

Not being a religious person there could be no comfort taken with thoughts of heaven. I did not embrace the thought of long lost loved ones lining up to greet me either. All I could know was that things as I knew them were ending and that I may never open my eyes again. Fascinated as I was with negativity, I could not have been prepared for what did greet me.

It began as a continuation of my death bed which was visits

either from the other side or their dreams. Images of other interactions occur as the current scene dissolves. I was a bit distraught for a few moments, then realized the journey was just continuing. It left a deep impression of hope, as I embraced death in completion.

The details of an evolution are personal. My only intent is to deliver the notice that death is not the enemy. Quite the contrary. It's easier, however, if you choose not to fear it.

I guess that's it.

****

14

Smallpox

Dear friend,

It was a misty morning in the fields. A dampness clung to the air making a deep breath more of an effort. As I watched a droplet of dew trickle down a dogwood leaf I felt a nonfamiliar tightness in my chest. It was only a moment, which was shrugged off by the amount of work that lay before me.

My hired hand still coming from behind the house left me to start by myself. I paid no never mind after that one moment. Too much to do with so little time. We had at least four tree trunks to split before the day would be done. I chopped through all of it while Tom, my hand, split the pieces for firewood. With winter so close on our heels it was critical to have all of it next to the house before the first bite of frost. After that the wood would be harder to chop….. so we got to it.

It took most of the whole day. Even with Tom trading spots we were still both spent by the end of the day, our arms heavy with the repetitive motion.

My wife Ellen had stew ready for us at sunset. It was wonderfully hot with pork and vegetables. She had had a busy day herself of preparing our crops for winter food. She was a hard working woman one of whom made me proud to be with her abilities to survive. "Hardy stock!" as my father would have put it. I loved her my whole life but now it was more of an appreciation than a lust.

The sun was just behind the barn when I felt the tightness in my chest again. My arms felt heavy but I figured that the strain of chopping was settling into my bones. Nothing that a good night's sleep wouldn't fix.

I pulled the quilt up to my chin, feeling suddenly very cold. A dull ache in my forehead began to pound. Ellen went to the well to wet a cloth to make me feel better, but to no avail.

Throughout the night I grew colder then hotter. It was a fever for sure that gripped me tightly by the throat. My greatest hope was that that was all it was, and not something more dangerous. My muscles ached fiercely but I clung to the idea it was from the over work. My head was aching the next morning followed by nausea. It was nothing more than influenza I declared. I suggested isolation but Ellen would hear none of it. The next few days were important she declared. I needed nursing and she would be the one to give it. I had learned many years ago not to argue with her, besides, I felt so sick I could barely move my head off the pillow. Whatever this was….. it was bad.

It took about four days of agony before the rash appeared. The feet and face followed before the bumps started to fill with fluid. I heard the intake of breath from Ellen before she whispered "small pox". In my fevered head the word had no meaning. The fire inside continued to burn as I felt my soul take flight to escape the heat. It ravaged through my bloodstream burning everything in its path.

The only clear moments were outside my body. I would drift out watching dear Ellen with her remedies in her lap. I wondered why she had not fallen ill. Surely the fire had begun long ago now. She did not cry but held my blistered hand to her chest. I could feel her warmth but it was not enough to entice me back to that body.

I was fine with the idea of no return with regards to myself.

I wondered for Ellen and her safety.

I suppose I hovered for longer that I should have, contemplating how I could help her.

Ellen pulled the quilt up over my blemished face. A sigh of sorrow as she stepped away. I decided to wait for her until she is ready, as the smallpox this time has seen fit to pass her by.

***

15

So This Is What It's Like To Be Transitioned

Dear friend,

I vaguely remember those last moments of pain. In the blur of morphine the struggle to hang on seemed impossible. My hand grasping reality only to find it sifting through my fingertips like sand.

Acceptance of death as a final act was always a topic I adhered to. It all seemed a fairytale set up to aleve the fears of children and the fearful. Finality was a comfort for a disassembled life that was not easy to embrace. So in other words I was welcoming the end.

Despite the popular notion of a universe created by God, I stood by my conviction that he/she was a lie as well. All nice and neat, the escape from the pain was really my only focus. The mantra of "more, more, more" the final cry of release. The "more" of course being the morphine that had become my savior in those final moments.

It did not occur to me at first that I had shifted my focus. I mean "passed on". Since I expected nothing to encounter, something was definitely disconcerting.

So if there was something, was there a "God" as well?

I turned over in my bed, an act not possible in the past few weeks, and stared at the ceiling. Shadows danced before as the cars from the street drove by. The shapes gradually turned into images that I could walk into. Surly this was an hallucination from the drugs. It could not be real. I kept expecting a veil of darkness that would accompany oblivion..... it did not arrive. The shapes on the ceiling became shapes of familiarity that were also human in appearance. I recognized their faces as they smiled at me. This was not what I expected..... how could I have been so wrong?

Suddenly I was intertwined in the energy, leaving the hospital bed behind me. Images continued to rise before my eyes, offering an exhilaration I had not felt in a long time. Choices hovered in my eyeline. The unlimited becoming tangible in my thoughts. So this is what it's like to be transitioned. The concept startled me but settled into sensible awareness.

I could live again if I chose. Perhaps somewhere in time I will. Until then the universe is enough.

****

16

I Stood Up Without Remembering That Mom Had Been Dead For About Ten Years

Dear Friend,

It was during the silence that I realized that time did not really exist. A leaf danced away from me.

I could only open one eye, the other was smashed into the sidewalk, most likely to never see anything again. Normally a city street is filled with sound, but I could hear the beat of my heart only. It had a tribal pulse to it that felt extremely primal. I wanted to get up, dust myself off to continue my journey home.

I couldn't.

The feet before me not moving. The silence remaining.

From a distance I heard my name being called.

"Can you hear me?"

The words were coupled with a sudden sensation of being moved. I wanted to reply but there was no indication of who was speaking. It sounded familiar in my hushed state of existence.

There was a sharp jolt, but I could not distinguish where it came from.

I kept hearing the woman's voice calling my name. "Robert! Robert!"

It struck me as odd because anyone who knew me called me Bob. I even had it changed on my driver's license a few years back. Strange.

The silence was still, here like a waiting friend. Nothing had changed, but there should have been, because my mind knew that time should have passed..... but it didn't.

I heard the woman's voice again.

A sudden wave of energy filled me, and I managed to turn over on my side. Where was the voice coming from?

My rational mind thought it might be a paramedic or the like. It came closer and closer until I was looking in my mother's eyes. "Robert, I've been looking everywhere for you."

I stood up without remembering that Mom had been dead for about ten years. It didn't faze me. We simply began to walk away from the silence. It closed like a door behind us signaling the release of time as I knew it.

There was an accident behind us. Rumor said that someone got hit by a car. They were trying to resuscitate the poor guy. I hope it works out for him.

I continue the walk with my mother. Our destination isn't clear but we have much to catch up on.

****

17

What Do You Bring With You?

Dear friend,

"What do you bring with you?" the sphere of light inquired. In my confusion the answer escaped me entirely. I did not even have my physical form, so what could the question mean?

In the preceding moments I had had quite a lot. So the question was misleading, for I felt like someone who suddenly found themselves without their wallet.

Grasping for any type of answer I replied, "Nothing." A short reply but the only one that came to mind under this situation. I felt like a child in the midst of reprimand. The sphere of light seemed to melt into a human face. I suppose it was my own mind creating the form but it really looked like someone. I waited for a reply, but none was forth coming. I do not recall how long I stood there or if I was really standing. All the physics I had studied were suddenly meaningless. There was not ever recognition if there was an upright position.

So I will assume all is well. No focus on the laws of physics as I knew them. The light grows more defined and I swear the face appears amused. Is it me or my answer of "nothing"?

"What have you brought with you?" The sounds reverberate

and I still do not know. I had many things to bring, however they are of no meaning now. This place does not sustain physical things. I search my memories and there is nothing. Again I am asked. Again I say "nothing".

I feel sad, I feel that I could have brought something. Did I forget or did I just not see the importance? My mind a flurry of activity. I start to perceive the importance of bringing something with me. A lesson, a quote, a moment of love. These things can come with me.

I now understood. Let me return and I will try something. So I return to start over. With a new realization I evolve and I understand. I will write my thoughts on the next life pattern. Goodly, I must be reborn. It is time.

Samba Serrado

18

Four Words To Live and Transition By

Dear friend,

Everything I have ever known is wrapped up in this current existence. How do I define what is truth and what is a mere figment of my imagination?

I hover between death and life. The choice yet to be made between the two. It is difficult to arrive at a decision, but necessary to the whole picture.

Much easier it would be if there were real moments of both that could be combined. I miss those who I share love!..... and intimacy.

As I wait for the transition there is much thought given to the subject. I never perceived my current predicament. Anticipation of death was filled with predetermined images that gave definition to what I perceived as reality. Actually these thoughts were just a precursor to the totality of my whole thought process. Having been accused in other lifetimes of being extremely boring. I bow to the possibility that all of it is pure bunk!

However, when I see the starlight on a darkened sky I am always taken by the huge possibilities that may be occurring right under my nose. Reality seems vast but actually the most personal relationship you may have.

Wherever you find yourself, whether it be at the bottom or the top, you have placed yourself there. By taking responsibility you empower yourself beyond measure. Be bold in your perceptions of the self. Know your power.

Now I continue the wait in this place of personal power. I am one with my thoughts. Basking in the knowledge that I am indeed the artist.

Understand. Know. Be. Evolve. Four words to live and transition by. We wait until the blending is complete. The change coming quickly, but not without great thought.

We are gladdened by the search as we go peacefully to the next arena.

****

19

The Velocity Of The Impact Killed Me Instantly

Dear friend,

Life passes you in the blink of an eye. Or perhaps even less if you are not paying attention. In my last life I spent a great amount of time worrying about the future. When I was a child it was not always so, but as maturity set in so did the focus pattern that would follow me my whole life.

I could detail the beginning but it would have more impact if I started at the end. By then my life was spiraling out of control. Of course I could not identify it, but it was truthful all the way.

It started (the end that is) on a Monday afternoon just before rush hour. In my haste to be onto the next thing, I had left the office early hoping to avoid traffic.

My day had been full of phone calls and deals. Deals that I thought would impact my future better. Faxes, emails, call waiting and cell phones dominated my existence. I was in a rush to the freeway when the tractor/trailer crossed the median and hit me head on. It would have been less fateful if I had not been driving so fast. However, the velocity of the impact killed me instantly.

I had wondered once if death would hurt. It did….. a little. The effect was not prolonged and the memory not first in my remembering of the event. My skull was crushed. Fascinating when you view it from another perspective. The roar of fire engines and the meticulous way the investigators examined the scene gave off somewhat of a circus atmosphere. I felt like I sat on the guard rail for days. The accident was almost cleared before it dawned on me. "What was I supposed to do now?"

In the back of my mind there were stories of angels and Pearly Gates. The edge of the highway offered no such visions for me. The light of the day faded away leaving me in the occasional glare of a passing motorist's headlights. Everyone rushing in so many different directions. Could they see me? My body had been taken away some time before, but myself as I knew it still sat by the roadside.

Losing time perspective is an odd thing. I could have sworn that I had been there for hours. My watch, or what I thought was my watch, indicated it had been about three hours since the accident. Since no one had taken notice of me I decided to walk home. It was in a slower pace that I noticed things I never did before. For example, the toll booth guy looked tired. I had seen this guy numerous times over the last year, but never looked at his face. I wondered why. Halfway down the freeway, I noticed a habitat for wildlife. Who had put it there? I had no memory of its existence. All the way to my house I found numerous things that did not appear to be there when I was alive.

Upon arriving home I saw that the authorities had beaten me there. The flashing red light had attracted a few of the neighbors. My wife could be seen in the window, her head in her hands. She was crying.

I wanted to stop everyone to tell them I was there. I felt okay. There must have been a huge mistake. Everyone was moving about so quickly. Why were they moving so fast and not paying attention? In frustration I screamed my name as loud as I could. Again no luck.

As I turned away I noticed a guy sitting calmly in an old Rambler across the street. He sat very erect on the hood of the car looking it seemed, directly at me. I walked down towards him hoping he could see me. As I got closer he smiled. "Pretty crazy, huh?!" he said.

Wow! Someone saw me. I did still exist.

A thousand questions tumbled from my lips. He merely smiled and held up his hand.

"You used to vibrate much faster than these individuals. How does it feel to be invisible to the naked eye?"

All of a sudden, I understood. It was my turn to feel the actual difference of an out of control life. Moments ago I was just like them….. what an eerie feeling.

"Want to take a walk?" he asked.

"How about a slow walk?" I replied.

So there it was. Two non-physical beings slowly making their way to another time and space. There was no rush. No rush at all.

****

20

Everyone Has A Path

Dear friend,

I remember the thought of my grandmother's death. The process of her departure a grueling one for my family. At the time I was only ten years old. The idea of death and disease so foreign to my experience. I could see the deterioration of her body but was unable to translate it to mine. She was a big part of my childhood, always a participant in birthdays, holidays, and just everyday stuff. When It was over there was a big empty spot that never was filled again.

My mother soothed me with the idea that Grandma was up in heaven watching over us. It was a comfort at the time but as I grew older she was not as present. Perhaps it was my own doing. My life blossoming while taking up so much time. There were moments of remembrance but I so did wish that she had been part of my life in a more physical way.

My mother always held the belief that she would be with Grandma again. It took her through the bad times giving her the strength she needed to carry on with her children. As I grew older I understood that, especially when I had children of my own. In adulthood my religious beliefs altered to my point of view. The patterns established in my youth not as poignant for who I was becoming. Questioning the whole process led me away from the established faith of my family to my own path. My mother understood but held fast to her faith. We hardly spoke of it until she herself became ill. The sight of her ravished body bringing back those moments when I was 10 watching Grandma in her final fight.

In the quiet moments we spent together in the hospital I gently asked my mother if she truly believed she would see her mom again. In her weakened condition my mother miraculously pushed herself up onto her elbows. Her look so intent I was spell bound.

"I know I will see her again," she replied.

"Mom. Could it be because you were told to believe that by the church?" I replied.

Smiling, she began to speak.

"Honey, everyone has a path. Just because yours is a different one does not negate mine. Religion for me has helped me understand a lot of things, however, I know that it's not religion that will help me through this. It is my belief system. Thoughts are what makes it all work. When I go I will see grandma because she has lived in my thoughts all these years. Whatever form she takes I will be satisfied because I know she will be there. Just like we will for you."

With that she closed her eyes and laid back. I sat for a long time just holding her hand. My thoughts turning to my own children. What would I tell them about death? They were also fairly young, the idea foreign to them as well. My mother died early the next morning. The final breath came before I returned.

There was no disappointment, only curiosity if my mother was indeed with grandma. My decision to keep both of them consciously alive in my thoughts passed to my children. We daily spoke of them and to them, my daughter particularly benefitting from the exercise. I could see it in her eyes.

The years passed. I found myself laying in a hospital bed preparing for the moment. My daughter looking into my eyes allowed me to see my own mother and her mother reflected in them. I too knew they would be there. No religion attached. When I closed my eyes I felt a shift. Two pinpoints of light moved towards me. The energy felt familiar, however, there was no physical orientation. Even without that, I knew who and what they were.

"We can be anything we like," they whispered.

So I left with them. Knowing my daughter would follow some day.

We were blissful.

****

21

It Was A Bomb

Dear friend,

I saw it all happen like a slow motion thrill scene from a movie. In fact in the confusion I forgot for a moment that it was actually real. Sound was muffled, or was it because the slow movement of the time that I was not used to? My thoughts progressed as usual but the physical moments so slow I was able to memorize every detail.

It was a bomb, at least that's what my mind registered. There was a brief bright light like someone taking a flash photo to close to your eyes. It knocked me backwards into the wall behind my desk. The clunk of my head against it sent tingles down my spine. The view after the flash only memories now, but I saw the following things…..

My favorite plant danced to the now gone ceiling disappearing into oblivion. I wanted to reach up to pull it back. We had a history, that plant and I. It was given to me my first day in the office. Together we had unearthed a few dry spells….. now it was gone, bringing me close to tears.

I saw furniture blow by me completely out of control. If they hit anyone they were sure to be killed. What kind of power did it take an office chair with wheels through the air?

My head snapped back as it hit on the wall. I wondered where my purse was. There was Tylenol in there. My temples were pounding as I scrunched my toes trying to keep my shoes on. I had just bought them the previous week and was absolutely in love with them. The debate within about the price gnawing at me again because to lose them would be devastating.

The dirt in my eyes blinding me momentarily to the sight of Charles dissolving like a Star Trek character, interesting. I wonder where he was beaming up to? He would be a reluctant candidate for such an endeavor. Perhaps it's best that the choice was random, he did not have time to think about it.

I felt an intake of air that did not feel like oxygen. There was a burning sensation at the back of my throat. As I turned my head the idea of a cold bottle of water filled me. There was a mini refrigerator near the coffee maker. I made the decision to get a bottle but found the journey impossible. So forceful the energy pushing me away, the searing burn growing larger down my throat. My stomach burned as did my lungs. The art of breathing painful beyond words.

I feel lifeless. My arms heavy with a burden I cannot identify. All I know is that it is heavy.

I strain to see if there is anything left of the place I knew. In my head it's all still there. The sameness of it and its occupants give me comfort in the chaos. I hear screaming in the distance. Am I screaming too? If I am does anyone hear me?

I remember my purse, thinking that I should call home to tell my husband that there may be a delay. Was there any mention of this on the news? No need to worry, I am all right. My greatest concern is my plant that disappeared a while back. What will I defrost for supper? There was a lamb stew I made a few Sundays back. That would be great after a day like today. Hopefully we won't be asked to stay overtime to clean up this mess. I haven't been this tired in a long time. Part of me is wishing I had stayed home today. I believe it would have been better that I did.

I feel myself afloat on a raft in a large swimming pool. The bobbing of my body against the wall almost a lullaby for my stressed thought process. The sun beats down upon me and I wonder if I put enough sunscreen on. If I stay in the sun there could be a nasty burn.

My mother calls me for supper. Her voice exactly the same tone and pitch it was twenty years ago. I sigh a disappointed breath a little frustrated that she called me so soon. She knows how I hate to end my day at the pool.

Paddling to the side I pull myself up. Dinner is waiting but I can't resist one more dive off the diving board. The water wraps itself around me. The heat of the sun dulled by the water and its reflection. I dry myself quickly because I hear the impatience in Mom's voice. I take one more look at the pool knowing I will return for a dip another time. It does not dull the disappointment, but the anticipation of another day soothing.

I remember something about a plant lost in the subtle moments of daydreaming. Another thought released to the sky only to return when I choose to remember. I hear her voice again, a little more agitated this time, calling me to dinner. The explosion now only a depression in a timeline unrelated.

Did I die?

I am not certain.

I don't remember.

Did I cry out in pain?

I don't remember.

Was I dreaming of an office that exploded?

I don't know.

Do I remember the details?

Yes.

Does it make a difference now?

No.

All I know is that my mother is calling me to dinner and I better move quickly. She hates to be kept waiting.

A flutter of ash glides slowly through the pockets of air on its way to the ground. All that's left of a physical form once known as Marcy. Is that all there is of a woman who was a vice president of a company? Is there such little meaning in the physical that it cannot translate beyond this vibration? Is she annihilated?

All that the universe can tell you is that Marcy is on her way to dinner with her mother.

The remnants of this life dissolved into the most important moment….. my mother.

On my way to meet her I feel excitement. Perhaps together we can move onto new experience. Nothing is ever lost, only translated to another frequency.

****

22

I Left Life With A Bitter Taste in My Mouth

Dear friend,

I left life with a bitter taste in my mouth, shouting words that now have no meaning. The finality so great I shudder with a chill that goes to my core. The knack for creating such animosity a familiar pattern though I was unable to identify it before now.

Deep regret fills me as I sift through the dramatic displays of my existence. Twisted and peppered with ugly superlatives. The words live on in a pattern that can now never be altered. The damage complete I move between the moments awaiting another linear opportunity.

One always believes in the infinity of the moment while youth pulses in one's veins. The idea of finite altered by blind ambition to live one's life. In those brief moments of clarity the mind attempts to adjust. However, the battle usually lost to stimulus of impulse. I recall the time lost but float now amongst the debris of several lives, all it seem belong to me.

The potential of communication not expected, but opportune for a soul such as I. The lingering a provision created by my regret of your mistreatment.

An apology even now in my distorted state. The idea forms of another setting so that all of the chaos of my thoughts may be resolved.

In an effort to be clear I wipe the haze of indifference from my eyes. The sight of poor choices mingled with my victimhood reflects vividly. I wish it to change but the uncertainty blocks my progress.

If we should encounter each other again my fervent wish would be to reconcile the negativity of my actions. Know that I regret our final interaction.

It does not reflect my true feelings. Please forgive me.

I also need to forgive myself.

****

23

I Guess I Share My Thoughts In The Hope That Someone From My Family Stumbles Across It

Dear friend,

I never felt it. By the time it went through my body the consciousness within my brain left. The biggest surprise was the observance of the aftermath. It's amazing to watch one's self without the self present. At first I did not recognize the face I inhabited for almost thirty years. Serene. Yes, serene is how I would describe it. The absence of energy truly identifiable immediately.

The police came quickly rolling the body on its back. I always thought crime scenes were left untouched. Evidence being the most important part. Maybe they thought I was still alive. I don't know. It seemed impossible from my viewpoint. How they held out any hope is remarkable, or maybe they were just non-observant.

As they put the body on a stretcher to take it away, I felt no remorse. A detachment had developed. So focused upon the body removal has left me rather uninformed. All I can see in this moment is the end result of being gunned down. God! I should be more upset, however, I am not.

The surroundings resemble a mist covered environment, sort of like a foggy morning.

Curiously the disassociation from my body has not affected my memory of events. If I think about it, participation in that life remains vividly as a matter of fact. (My rampant thought process is attempting to wrap my head around that one.)

My family is foremost now in my thoughts as the formal memorial process has begun. Funny how quickly time has moved past the fatal event. Suddenly I was witness to those saying goodbye.

I'm not lost to them. They will remain in my heart eternally. I believe their tears are more for themselves than me. I definitely do not need sadness. I feel a moment of transcending occurring, though the origin and destination are still forthcoming.

I guess I share my thoughts in the hope that someone from my family stumbles across it. The shooting was random. Though I remember having an inkling of its occurrence. I never felt it.

Honest.

I now walk deeper in the mist. Images are beginning to form and my curiosity is getting the better of me.

Adieu.

We shall see you again.

By then I will have new experiences to share.

****

24

Something Was Definitely Different

I had given up hope of ever feeling well again. Each day was a struggle just to get through. The barrage of pills lining my night stand ticked off the hours. A blue one at ten, a pink one by noon and two yellow ones by two in the afternoon. Keeping it all straight a dire task that I chose to ignore whenever possible.

My lack of commitment to the medication schedule prompted the hiring of a nurse. Comparable to a Fraulein in Nazi Germany, she dispensed it all with a no-nonsense attitude. I resented the imposition upon my freedom of choice. After all, no one suffered but myself with the neglect. It was only to satisfy my adult children that I agreed to the situation.

I contemplated the freedom of my beliefs of a hereafter imprinted from childhood slowly eroding with each painful day. If there was a God, why did he allow this horrible suffering? Was I that much of a sinner that a "hell on earth" was necessary for my situation?

In my mind I became weary of the search for answers. The truth was that the pain would never go away. A heavenly respite doubtful because that would imply there was a god. I, through the haze of pills, suspected that there wasn't.

So it continued.

An endless circle of agony from which the only deliverance was death. Under the watchful eye of the Nazi, I was kept alive with my torment. Why couldn't it just be over and done?

It was inevitable, I suppose, that I would lose track of time the way that others perceived it. The punctuation coming only from the pills as they were administered. It was such a pointless exercise. There would be no redemption of the flesh.

No.

None at all.

It was after the blue pill of the night sky that something changed. At first I thought I was dreaming, but the presence of the Nazi nurse quelled all hopes of that. She took my water cup without comment, which was odd. She always capped our exchanges with "Thank you Mr. Feldman". I felt relief from the sameness by her neglect.

I felt a tingle in my fingertips that crawled up my arms like a chill. The pill traveled slowly down my throat, implying more water was needed. I reached for the water glass by my bedside hoping to wash it down. To my surprise, the tightness in my throat subsided. The tingle in my fingers ceased abruptly, the feel of the glass suddenly having no structure. For a moment I sensed that this was just another "loss" I would have to deal with. Anger burned in the pit of my stomach while I contemplated about what to do next. Interesting how emotion stimulates and reacts to thought.

Something was definitely different, however, I was unable to define what it was. I declined to ring for the nurse, not sure I was able to deal with her. Placing the glass back on the nightstand I began to piece together what the difference was. I was not in pain! The absence of it was subtle yet explosive. My thoughts no longer dulled by the persistent nag of it. My room expanded before me in the realization of what had occurred.

My pain was gone….. was I still alive?

Of course I was. The pure result of what I was experiencing was that I was indeed still alive. Was it one of the pills that pushed me over the edge? Or was it a divine intervention from a merciful god after all?

I slid out of bed and went to the window. The sun was just beginning to peek over the horizon. What a beautiful sight it was. I had forgotten what it looked like. To think that it happened with certainty every day without my witnessing it….. what a waste!

Every step I took to the window was a miracle. I couldn't recall the last time I had been vertical. The return of the nurse would no doubt spoil everything. In the meantime, I gazed at the rising sun with thankfulness.

The light of the sun grew brighter. It was so enticing that I found myself desiring to walk into its warmth. I looked around my room that had been a prison for so long.

It took but a moment to make the decision. If this was death it was a welcome sight. If it wasn't, then there was nothing to lose. It's just that it wasn't what I was expecting.

In an act of defiance I swept away the array of pills at my bedside. I would take no more pills.

I stepped into the window frame, removing the latch as I did so. Remarkable how well I felt. The light grew brighter with each movement towards it.

I never looked back.

****

25

My Astonishment During The Transition

Dear Friend,

Outside from the fact that this correspondence ability is absurd, I feel the potential that it could occur. My whole existence was rooted deeply within tradition. Every moment had structure into a pre-subscribed order set down by all those who had lived before us. To believe the death experience to be anything other than completion simply incorrect. I should know, I instituted much of the doctrine living my life as others dictated.

There can be no preparation for death other than anticipating the inevitable by just living. Sooner rather than later, a good mindset.

My astonishment during the transition silencing my usual acid tongue. Instead of annihilation I was submerged into a lullaby of comfort intertwined with a stream of highly intellectual consciousness. My awestruck being realizing in that moment how wrong I had been.

How unfortunate that the life lived was wasted in my denial. The lost evolution a consequence of a closed mind. The unlimited perspective I now participate with beyond even a gullible expectation.

No matter what you decide, know that it is possible to be wrong in your belief system. Death is the beginning. I, of all who have faced it thought differently. I acknowledge the error while moving forward to participate with new parameters.

Perhaps there will be a difference in what is accomplished.

****

26

Did I Mention My Name?

Dear Friend,

I kind of come apart when thinking about it, this moving on stuff. It was not something that should happen so soon, especially if you're a guy or gal with plans. Yeah. Lots of plans that you could put money on. They were gonna be great. Ask anyone who knew, they'd tell ya. That Frances boy, he had a lot, was gonna do something, always said he would.

My Mama was my biggest supporter. She made sure I did not dawdle on some corner with nothing to do. After we lost Papa she made sure of it. Most times as a kid we'd fight about it, but she always won out. She was one tough broad, my Mama.

I started working in my uncle's bakery when I was fourteen sweeping up, helping customers and generally being an errand boy. Small potato stuff it was. Like I said, I had bigger plans. Did I mention my name? It's Francis. Well it became necessary to toughen up a bit. I changed it to Frank. My close buddies called me Franco. The neighborhood my oyster, was a great place for a guy with plans. By day in the bakery. By night at the gin mill by the corner. That was where a regular guy like me could make a few coins, especially on a Saturday night.

So where was I?

A punk kid with no idea of what it feels like to die. All I care about is either in a beer or my pants. I can do what they ask. I get it all. Know what I mean?

So I tell Mama I'm working the later shift. It starts real early like two in the morning. Perfect, because that's when the action starts. Instead of making crème puffs I'm sinking real corn in my shoe. I get there just when it's starting to rain. Doesn't matter to me. I just have to get the package and get out. Done it twelve times from Sunday. No problem.

I pull my collar up around my neck since the wind picked up. Didn't want to have to explain why I was sneezing to Mama.

So this guy pulls up, a real dandy type. I take about two steps before he shoots me. No reason. The lousy bum just opens up with the lead. Now I'm on the pavement with my guts in my hands, wondering how I was gonna explain this. The car pulls away fast choking me on the exhaust.

What a rat!

How was I gonna collect the dough now?

My head felt light like the time I chugged some tequila in the alley with Joe and Marty. I was afraid to stop holding my belly cause everything might fall out or something. Wish there was a cushion for my head.

I see these shoes right by me. That would be all I need. A wise guy to beat my brains out while I'm down. The luck just keeps pouring in.

So I close my eyes waiting for the worst, but nothing happens. These huge hands come under me, lifting me to my feet. Finally, a good Samaritan or the like. Imagine my surprise and horror to my old man standing there.

It took a few minutes to realize that he shouldn't be standing there.

"Let's go," he said gruffly.

Go?

Go where old man?

I had to get home before Mama woke up. Didn't I?

"Never mind about all that. Your Mama be here soon enough. If I were you I'd be wishing she'd take her time," said Papa as he walked from me.

I followed, torn up by what had happened. Too late to change it.

I followed him down the street. There was nothing left to do but move on.

****

27

I Watched With Detachment As They Took My Old Body Away

Dear Friend,

It's a unique experience looking at yourself from the outside in. Admittedly there was no preparation for what was seen. At first there is a disbelief as one hovers overhead and gazes upon the face it knows so well. There is a lack of connection because I believe there is a difference in the look without the spirit that views it.

My thoughts were calm as I watched, which surprised me a great deal. There should have been some sort of distress involved or at least a mild panic. However the separation was no more alarming than a dream, though I was aware I was not.

I wondered what the implications would be if I stayed separate? Would the body simply die from the lack of connection to my energy? Or would it continue as a breathing receptacle for another energy should it pass by?

Since this had all occurred while I slept in my bed, would there be enough time to call paramedics? And if there was enough time did I really want to trade this tranquility for my stressful previous environment?

Mary Ellen slumbered beside me in the bed, her auburn hair

spread across her pillow like a halo. She was indeed an angel throughout our marriage.

From this viewpoint there was nothing but love and affection for her though we had been fighting more often than not lately. Funny how I cannot even remember what the disagreements were about. Their importance diminished by the delicate outline of her face against the pillow.

So fascinated by these thoughts I step into a reenactment of many of them. None worthy of mention here on this page. Most silly dramas powered by my own insecurities and foolishness. Each however in retrospect giving me clarity in this particular moment.

A change of energy snaps me back to my observational position above my body. The sun has begun to peek through the curtain ever so faintly. I used to dread the mornings, for they signaled the end of my rest and the beginning of days that used to spin out of control.

The victimhood ever running rampant now causes me to laugh a bit as I realize that I was truly in control. How easy it was to blame pointing fingers at the culprits responsible.

I continue the review until Mary Ellen breathes deeply turning over to face me, or rather my body. She reaches out her fingers gently caressing the skin on my arm. Her eyes open abruptly as she realizes that something is amiss. I want to fold her in my arms as she calls my name to awaken me. I know the tone of her voice is one of fear. She reaches for the telephone for help.

Is it too late?

I wonder if it is or could I slip back without any notice?

The rush of energy from the paramedics is interesting. They carry a feeling of focus that is intended to save lives. However, attached to it is a feeling of been there, done that, which they wear as a protective shield. Dealing with crisis and death is a much more harrowing experience than I ever envisioned while living.

There it was, my acceptance of circumstance that I did not realize. There would be no return to the body, now under scrutiny by the paramedics. In realizing there was nothing they could do, I turned my attention to Mary Ellen who was by the door sobbing quietly.

Oh how I wished to be of comfort to her. It felt so important to reveal myself to her, but I did not know how. There was nothing on a physical level to do. Only in the giving of energy I could help her.

In her sadness she was impossible to reach. There was an armour-like quality to her that I understood was out of protection. The loss she felt beyond comprehension, but I understood. Now it was of the utmost importance to signal her in some way. But how?

I could feel a magnetic pull of my energy as I stayed beside her. There was not an inkling of desire to move forward yet. My focus deeply upon her throughout the episode.

I watched with detachment as they took my old body away. It was not the me I knew anymore. I was here fully engaged in the pattern occurring. My hand firmly on the shoulder of my wife as she passed zombie like from room to room.

Fortunately she was surrounded by friends and families who provided limited distractions to ease her grief. Mary Ellen was a strong woman. I knew given the right combination, she would pick herself up and live on. My intention was to stay close until that moment came.

It is said that "time heals all wounds". In my current state I feel that it should be changed to "connection heals all wounds of body and soul".

My connection with my wife has healed her loneliness. She still pines for my physical presence. I know she feels my energy every moment. Communication is limited due to the difference of our current existences, but there are brief encounters that we both cherish.

I await my Mary Ellen, her time moving towards her. This not but a brief interlude to our revisiting in spirit. The body merely a vehicle along the way.

I still watch her sleep, the delicate features forever etched in my thoughts. When it's available we meet in her dreams to continue our relationship.

Yes, it's quite possible. I can relate to your skepticism, but it's undeniably true. In your position you are more focused, or so you believe in you waking hours. However your sleep cycle is just as valid.

I await our reunion with more clarity. Our next enactment perhaps more connected as the lessons of this one permeates our consciousness.

****

28

The Chuck Wagon Was Low On Supplies For Weeks

Dear Friend,

I mostly remember the water in my boots. One of my stockings was full of holes so the water be flooding my toes with every step. It was no help that my boot was worn then by the rocky ground. We be marching on every day. Some days my feet be so cold I would forget what it is like to feel them. The cold go all the ways up to my knees most times.

The chuck wagon was low on supplies for weeks, leaving us with only beans and rice. I did not complain cause something was better than nothing. The grumbling grew fierce when it went on for so long. I was used to eating only to quiet the growling in my belly. Most of my unit were used to eating for pleasure. Most had mama's who cooked a full meal in good times. That was something I never had.

We came through the hollow near Richmond on a Sunday morning. I could almost hear the preacher in Jonesville giving his sermon of God. Every Sunday it echoed through my head. Just like a childhood memory I reckon. There was still dew on the ground when we started out.

I cursed when I felt my foot get wet again. The stocking had dried well near the fire that night before, so I reckoned I would have at least a few hours of warmth before we hit water.

My friend Alfred was next to me having a chuckle at my misfortune.

"Maybe we'll get some of those Yankees before sundown. If we get some I will share some new boots and socks."

"That is, if you will wear Union my friend."

He kept laughing, making me wish he would just stop flapping his jaw. His humor often grinding one when it went on for a spell. I spit some tobacco in his direction hoping for a direct hit. It fell short but when I was lookin at him, there was a blast. I watched Alfred drop dead in his tracks with blood dripping from the corner of his mouth. His eyes were on me as he slid to the ground.

The rest of us fell to the ground waiting for further assault. I crawled to my friend hoping to save him but by the time I get there, his eyes are seeing something else besides the hillside. He be mumbling about his family, but I can not make out what he say.

"Shhh! You gonna be fine." I lied as I witnessed his departure. Well maybe it not such a lie after all. Maybe he is fine. His body limp next to me on the ground. Shots bouncing off the trees filling the woods with sounds of death. There were four or five men down with our sergeant spurring us to regain our wits to retaliate against these bastards.

"Son of a bitch," A bullet came right across my face, barely missing my head. I lay low to the ground with my eyes closed. Maybe it just stop.

I hear the command to charge. My hands are shaking but I am not afraid. At least I don't reckon so. I hear gunshots with Union soldiers gaining ground. I tell myself to get up and fight but it be like I know it's useless. I see men falling to the ground. They have more fire power than us. If I stand, I will die like a man. If I lay here I am a coward. I know my daddy would be proud if I became a man. But, am I brave enough? Shutting my eyes I find the courage to face certain death. There is no time to wonder about it. I stood slowly, ducking my head to the gunshots. For courage I began to yell from my gut as if the sound will carry me to the gates of heaven. As I run I hold my bayonette in front of me as if there is hope I will not be shot. If I die I must die as a man.

It's all I have left.

A bullet hit the side of my neck. I was surprised at its force because it shot me back about four feet before I hit the ground. I began to swallow blood before I felt any pain. I began to think about home, wondering if my sister was still staying on there with my father. Since I never knew my mama, she was the closest thing to it. When my head hit the ground it didn't even hurt. By then I was mostly swallowing the blood as fast as I could. The feeling of smothering something I did not want to do.

I could hear the moaning of my unit. I guess they were all hit by this time. I kept my eyes on the sky still wondering about my family. There is a tin type in my shirt pocket of my mama that I hoped would get back to my family. It was the only time I'd ever seen her. She die while birthing me.

The shots were silent and all that was left was the dying. It crept up on me slowly, my head getting light from the wound in my neck. The rest of me only cold and that damn wet sock still irritating me so much. I tried to reach down to pull it off but I couldn't feel my fingers anymore. A fine misty rain began to fall. I figured that soon all of me could be soggy so I stayed still.

The smell of dirt and blood was everywhere but I did keep my eyes on the sky. It gave me comfort for reasons unknown to me.

I could hear commotion but it didn't matter, as I began to float towards the sky. There was someone in the distance but maybe I was dreaming. I did not know. I waited to see who it was. It looked like Mama but I never seen her before up close, only in the tin type. I struggled to reach in my pocket, but I couldn't get it.

I waited until she got closer. I could feel the life pouring out of my wounded body. I walked to her ready to know for sure. It was her allright. I left the battlefield a victim, but arrived victorious to the after life with Mama.

My feet ain't wet anymore.

****

29

I Have Taken My Own Life

Dear Friend,

The sun embraced my weary heart when I sat myself finally in the chair. So depleted of spirit the relaxation not occurring with out some deep inner direction.

Emotional outbursts endured while within, not surprising if one had any perception of my life thus far. The sheer hopelessness that enveloped me leaving a prolonged nausea that could not be contained.

With my eyes closed, the heat of the rays slightly burning the epidermis. I contemplate how I will do it. These thoughts find a familiar path as they tread into the corridors of my mind.

If not for cowardice the deed would have already existed. Some say that those who herald their impending doom never fulfill the wish. Falling so far into that category I begin to internalize the plan.

Who should be blamed for a life gone awry?

The siblings? The girlfriend?

Or simply the one who lives it? The debate runs rampant inside of my projecting a conclusion that gives no comfort. Trapped in my own illusion. I slide slowly to the moment necessary to end it once and for all.

Not an advocate of eternity, the annihilation of all redemptive probabilities my comfort. There is nothing else so the ending of the nightmare my final gift to myself.

Swallowing the pills in the sunlight takes the edge off the darkness that overwhelms me as I stumble out of this life. Yes. I intended to walk out. I expected the end to embrace me in a final dance. It was my belief that there was an oasis of nothing that would leave me finally in peace.

My pulse slowing until the breath became shallow. All of the pain diminishing while the pills did their deed. The eyes taking a final look before closing in anticipation of nothingness. At last, at last, release from my woes, never again to plague my weary heart.

A buoyant feeling taking one deeper into the abyss of annihilation that I so desperately desired. The warmth of the sun replaced with a chill of death, I welcomed the moment. Surely the end would come upon my countenance quickly so desperate I was to escape my bitter life.

The surprise at not embracing the infinite nothingness catching me off guard. Disappointment flooding me as the realization of a full destination unfolding, whatever this was it was not annihilation.

Did I not take enough pills? Surely the combination lethal to the taker, the data favoring demise. What place was this that my body had no recollection of the event.

I was whole, untethered and healthy.

The mind can wander aimlessly when in a disturbed environment. Was this it?

Was I dead without complete demolition?

The complexity of this event confusing for one who contemplated a direct path. It appeared that though my belief systems disallowed it, I had embarked on a path to eternity. It was not anticipated so, a backup agenda not forth coming.

A sensing of others equally unsettling as I moved through the space. Face materializing from nowhere, smiling in a most pleasant way.

Unable to resume the cold pattern of dismissal I wait for a word from this now materialized man.

“Who are you?” I asked stupidly. “Never one to believe,” I said with conviction.

“There are many things you believe you do not have. I simply come to show you the way” he said.

“I can’t get into heaven with you” I said softly. “I’ve taken my own life.”

“All the more reason for guidance” he said.

What if I just want to be annihilated?” I retorted.

You merely sought release from the pain” he said. “That I can help you with.”

“You have no idea what I want” I cried.

There was a stirring of emotion inside me that left an uncomfortable sensation. I did not anticipate this conversation, yet I felt it had played out before.

“Yes this has happened just this way before” he said, reading my mind. “You are caught in a cycle. Let me help you on your way.”

“I want out” I cried.

“Then allow it. Follow me” he said. The darkness began to lift. The decision beginning to shadow the viewpoint radically.

So I trailed behind this man who claimed to by my friend. All hopes of annihilation receding into the dark passages until another opportunity, why not?

Or why? Not comprehending I took the coward’s way out and did nothing. Will the identical events surround me on the next venture? I will not speculate. I’m just participating since it appears annihilation is not an option.

****

30

It Never Occurred To Me That I had Died

Dear Friend,

It has taken what has seemed as eons to understand my predicament. The voices start softly drifting off into a rhythm that often lulls me to sleep while thinking. You might ask what I think but then again you may be caught up in your own dramas so much it doesn't make a difference. Remembrance of such times filter through the thoughts making me realize how the connection all works.

I remember being hurt, the pain so exhausting. I wanted to die. Any relief was sought in the early moments. The shock running through my torso rampant in its destruction. My focus was to make it stop any way possible. When it did there were no questions, only the sigh of relief from a woman deeply grateful for the reprieve. The cycle continued half aware that I was of the circumstance. There might have been total acceptance without the presence of the voices.

They began as a heartbeat which was presumed as my own. The cadence alternating between my perceptions and those who were speaking. The rhythm remarkably comforting while I rested. Visions or should I say dreams swirled around me. All of it so natural with no inkling of repetition. The voices growing louder but unnoticed.

Perhaps this pattern would have existed indefinitely, certainly it was comfortable. It was the voices singing a distant melody that cut into the fiber of my creation. Making it less palatable, more confining. As they became clearer there was struggle to decipher the code in which they appeared to be speaking. It took my focus off my surroundings causing them to waver slightly. Those moments created questions that I felt certain could be answered by the voices. In all these moments it never occurred to me that I had died.

So soothing and pain free of an environment tempted me to put all considerations later. All I desired was the pain free calmness I was experiencing. Anything else could bring back all the pain. I suppose that was the reluctance I was feeling.

"Wake up" came the whispers, becoming louder and clearer. Over and over they chanted to me while wrapped in my blanket of creation. "Wake up and harken to your next place" they began to repeat. I lifted my head from my pillow of comfort, wary of what might be painful. There had been enough of it with no wish to return.

My eyes out of focus expecting the hospice bed and did not quite grasp what was before me. It must be the morphine but in the end it did not work. Only the delusion of chemical reaction did it give me, never the comfort that was felt now.

Did I want to leave my cocoon? Warily I gazed upon this place. There were many smiles from faces, some I knew, others vaguely familiar. All of them overjoyed at my attention.

"Welcome" said the chorus, again the melody I had heard for so long. So this is what I had heard.

The idea of death an odd one now that I am here amongst those who love me. My desire for release overcoming my desire to expand now unencumbered by my fear of pain. It is no longer part of me.

****

31

I Embrace A New Horizon

Dear Friend,

It seems my body has betrayed me. The focus of my thoughts has always led to the belief I create my reality. Why then, would it defy the intent, which clearly does not want the disease?

The many books on the subject declare that it is brought upon us by ourselves. An unbalanced energy pattern wreaking havoc upon a pristine system of life.

I rose from a deep slumber to find myself hostage to another spasm of pain. They told me it would worsen, however I did not expect this.

Meditating releases some of it but my mind unable to accept what is occurring, fights. The struggle deepening the torture until my eyes are full of tears.

How humiliating it is to encounter the fearful side of your psyche only to succumb like a blithering fool. My embarrassment at not being able to heal myself truly devastating.

I feel the slipping of essence for this physical body. There is nothing to reverse the momentum once it has declared its direction.

So I wait.

Wondering what will occur and who I will encounter. It creeps through me slaying all, taking no hostages.

Uncomfortable has become the goal from inconceivable. I search for release, the present showing me to the future.

Once the moment of no return arrives there is not a choice to be made. The release of my spirit with gladness. A moment of respite declared sublime.

The need to create a better physical form. Or at a minimum one that responds to thought more profoundly.

A fluid space of being prepares my consciousness for the next endeavor. An increase of focus brings it all into view. In my mind the in-between moment moves quickly, reinforcing my perception of evolving existence.

Since it never ceases in its perpetual dance, I relax into the rhythm of its intent.

The pain fades to nothing. My focus now clear. I embrace a new horizon, taking with me the ideas of creation.

****

32

I Write This To Let My Brother Know My Status

Dear Friend,

I hear your voice though my voice of response escapes me. Your questions are unanswerable for I know not the answers. A struggle ensues but I find myself on the losing end of the stick. Answers wade while all still ask "What is this place of my being?"

Come back you ask, no it's more like pleading. The urgency emanates from your heart. I feel it. I know it. The inability to reverse this process devastating.

Where am I? Not known for the moment, however I endeavor to find out. Your voice propels me to memories of our childhood when we were more at odds than harmony. Oddly those times clearly impact me in ways I have not considered. Our experience fruitful upon examination. I suspend myself in observation, becoming lost in boyhood antics with a brother who was more like me than I had known.

I still hear you. The melody of your voice patterns intoxicating. It all reminds me of our family and friends and yes children. Though we have not had them in this place, there is a memory. Too difficult to dissect, I move away towards what I believe is your self.

The struggle to maintain focus becoming more difficult. Nothing is solid. The vapor of thought sifting through a mesh which must be where you are. You might have to be braver than you'd like. The probability of finding enough stability to return less viable while writing this.

If I am writing it my thoughts created the idea of writing a letter to let you know my status. There's no guarantee it's actually occurring.

Just so you're kept informed. Know that, even if the return becomes null and void. I'm here. The destination remains cloudy but it occurs to me that I might have to let go to move. So I decide full participation is the only route. Know I take all of our interactions with me as a treasure. A genuine gift that changed me on this path.

Keep your heart beating, there's more for you here, so you should stay.

****

33

"Just Crossed Over, Have You?" He Asked

Dear friend,

All I wanted during those last moments was relief. A break from the constant pain that seemed to fill my every waking moments.

Nothing seemed to help anymore. So many potions and pills had passed my lips over the past few months. It would be impossible to recount them all to you. The only constant was the pain.

I can't blame anyone, they all tried in vain to help me. Doctors, it seems don't all know that much after all. I felt like a gamble to them. It was full of....

"I'm not sure."

"Let's try this."

"It appears to be making progress."

"Blah, blah, blah."

As I said before I just wanted relief. My mind was ready to

snap from it. All I believe I willed my self gone just to make it stop. It never occurred to me that I would not be able to get back.

That last night surrounded by my loved ones. I gripped their hands for support. The medication timeframe was going on and on. I watched the clock, hoping it would speed up to the next scheduled drip. It seemed like my whole life centered around the next dosage. They had given me the most intensity without damage so I was fairly at the end of my rope.

I'll admit I prayed for death quite diligently as a matter of fact. So when it actually occurred I was faced with the lack of pain but a great desire to return.

My thoughts were better placed without the distraction. Now in clearness the realization of leaving behind those I cherished left me desolate. I wanted to go back! I wanted to be with them. It felt like a tradeoff, this loneness for the pain. I felt cheated.

I could see all of them, including my body, gathered together in that hospital room. I could see the drip of medication, no longer such an important item, sitting by the bed.

No one could see me, nor feel me for what it was worth. It all felt so wrong. Was this all there was?

I watched it like an old movie. The colors vivid. The characters mourned their loss. Where were the angels I had heard about?

What of the Pearly Gate?

Granted, my one full wish of no pain fulfilled without doubt. The rest of it out of sync. The dots not connecting like I thought they would. I wanted to go back if this was it. Alas I did not know how.

A small old man approached the hospital room, his appearance vivid against the darkness. He looked ordinary, obviously another like myself lost to all with nowhere to go. He shuffled his feet over to me, his eyes looking at my family in grief.

“Poor old guy” he said shaking his head.

“What old guy?” I asked.

“Why that one” he said, pointing at my dead body in the bed.

“That’s me” I replied.

“Just crossed over have you?” he asked.

“Well I suppose so” I replied.

“What do you mean by that?” he said.

“Just doesn’t seem real, that’s all.”

While he spoke it dawned on me that this old man could see and hear me.

“Hey!” I exclaimed.

“Can you see me?”

“Not prone to talking to myself sonny.”

“Of course I can see you!” he said with irritation.

“You’re not inhabiting the form anymore. Not too quick are you?” he said looking me in the eye.

Stunned by his response I looked again at the body which I thought was me.

“But the pain?” I asked.

“Oh, if you really want to you can manifest it again.

Sometimes people do, sometimes they wise up and do something else."

"It's up to you friend!" he said, starting to walk again.

"What about my loved ones?" I asked, choking on a few tears.

"What am I? Chopped liver?" he replied.

"Grandma?" I said with surprise.

"It doesn't look like you?"

"Now you're starting to get it" he said, rolling his eyes that I should have recognized.

"To answer your question, I left it behind just like you are. It's an article of clothing, so to speak."

"So."

"Are you ready?"

I looked back at the hospital as the scene faded from view.

"They will be along, don't worry" he said with his hand on my arm.

"We'll meet them if you like."

"All right" I replied.

So I left behind the pain, the desire for relief and the dramas. As we moved, many things were suddenly available. That body wasn't me after all.

However, the little old man was most certainly the Grandmother I knew.

Why have you manifested yourself as a man?" I asked as we walked through galaxies.

"Just thought I would" she replied.

"Oh now I get it" I replied.

"It will get easier" she replied.

And I knew she was right.

****

34

I Write These Words With Hands That Are Not Solely Mine.

Dear Friend,

I write these words with hands that are not solely mine. The thoughts very much the me. I remember from physical, however, the "vehicle" long gone from existence.

The memory of that life still carries forward with me. All of the friends and family still important in my heart. I know that they feel me at certain times and wonder if it's really a connection or not. Their belief systems prohibiting the notion that we could actually converse if they liked. The idea that I am upward in a heavenly state is amusing. My existence is right next to you, the vibration being the only difference.

From this viewpoint I can perceive the future and parallel lives I heard about when I was physical. They do not appear in a line like one might think, rather all at once from all sides. I know you're thinking this spirit is mad indeed. Know many things now that may make me appear that way, but I am quite sane. There is a beauty to its existence that defines what we as people are. We incarnate and focus in a line for clarification and order. The memory of it fades once the body is no longer viable in linear terms than not. It's comparable to explaining to a blind man about color, very difficult.

We find it interesting to come through a physical form like this one. The memory of a possession fills us with laughter. It's not all that easy and the energy needed to keep it focused demanding. Most take a direct line of focus which requires pure energy. Those spirits of whom you would label as evil would not have enough pure energy to manifest, at least not for any great length of time. Therefore the perceived worry created by misinformed believe systems can be ignored in most instances.

I purely wanted to connect for the sole reason of opening possibilities. If there is opportunity for conversation there is an openness in my soul. I exist in the sideline of your manifestation. I will remain here until there is a discussion by myself to move on. For the moment I am content to take these small encounters and work with them.

I am very much like you even though my energy does not retain physical shape.

****

35

The Actual Event Proved To Be Anticlimactic On Many Levels

Dear Friend,

Isolated in my thoughts I write to you with the desire for clarity. Throughout my life concepts of life were presented that confused and manipulated my path. In the moment of presentation all of it appeared to have depth. Why else would everyone around me embrace it so?

A child's belief in his/her parent's perception of the world starts very young. There is no way to change the direction of the influence until adulthood is reached. By then the patterns ae fully established making it difficult to change.

My parent's concept of an all powerful god above them perplexes me. The structure of their lives centered around the trappings of religion that constructed their work, social and family circles.

My acceptance of this lifestyle while young gave way to hostile feelings of manipulation with the onset of puberty. The question of gods haunting me until my death.

A part of me anticipating the final moments, at last the questions answered. Would there be a wise St. Peter book of names in hand to guide me to my place, Happy Hunting Grounds? A ticket to another continuance of physical life? What?

I also wondered what the perception would be. Would I slip seamlessly without it missing a beat? Or would there be a struggle within the last moments, the desire to cling to be overpowering?

The actual event proved to be anticlimactic on many levels. Final breaths were labored but I found myself calm in spite of the lack of physical comfort. The pain just a slowing that spread from my heart to my extremities.

Knowing the moment was near I attempted to sit up for a final look. My feeble arms barely able to sustain for more than a second or two.

My room faded from view leaving momentarily at loss for a point of reference. Without my body a feeling of buoyancy overcame me. Did anything actually occur? Was I still living? The answer being affirmative to both questions. A line of perception took my sight to the corpse that remained. I was deceased.

Curiosity filled my thoughts and attempted to examine the physical man that I once knew. It barely resembles what I had stared at in the mirror for eighty years or so. There was no sense of remorse or attachment. Why should there be?

I felt my existence even more profoundly this moment than ever. I could feel the presence of others though there was not a manifestation of anyone. The surroundings cloudy resembling a rainy fog that inhibited my viewpoint. As the realization of my passing became clear, so did my perception of my surroundings.

Thoughts of my parents invading immediately. Through the cloudiness they emerged looking very much as they did in my childhood. Brief moments of euphoria followed as they embraced my heart.

Where were we? I asked expecting a revelation to be forthcoming. We are "in thought" they explained.

The old hostility returning without the explanation I so desperately needed. Everything they ever believed in now, seeming a cosmic joke. Or should I say a godlike joke?

"We were mistaken to have considered such narrow view. Thoughts propel us on the journey, not the other way around," they whispered.

What of the others still in physical? Were they doomed to find that everything they took for truth now a ridiculous falsehood?

Plunging into despair my mind began creating the surroundings, taking me on a grand journey through the life I just left. It occurred to me in this process that perhaps we are the god we seek. That through it all, it appears to be external when indeed it emanates from within.

So in my solitude I write this short essay to give you something to ponder. If we are gods then why the propaganda to believe otherwise.

Do not have feelings of despair for me. I can choose any reality I would like. The moment clearly calls for contemplation. I will create my own heaven in due time. The solitude is voluntary.

****

36

When My Death Arrived It Was Not What I Expected

Dear Friend,

I used to see nothing of interest on this alleged other side. The dribble of information passed to those hungry for continuation of their wretched lives. The reassurance sought left me wondering why everyone was so curious. I just did not believe that there was anything else. My opinion of those who desperately cling to the hope of more was blank.

Your time is your time. After that accept the fact that it's over. My whole family felt this way, which is probably why I fell into it so easily. When my death arrived it was not expected, especially by me. A freak accident that left me startled. I was alone on a highway changing a flat tire. I was greatly irritated by this inconvenience, coupled with the fact that I had awaited help that never arrived.

It had been awhile since I had to change a tire. The question of whether or not I had a spare crossed my mind. Checking the trunk I found that I did. A primitive jack was also there. So I started the process myself. The jack was not working so well at first. At closer inspection I saw that a part of it had rusted. Cursing, I pumped the handle with difficulty. A few cars went past, but they were hardly noticed while I concentrated on the tire removal.

I suppose it was ironic that just as I attempted to pull it off I slipped backwards. In the same moment a freight truck whizzed by knocking me quite roughly down the road. I remember the burning sensation as my skin brushed the pavement. I thought I was burning alive. I wanted to scream but couldn't, and then it suddenly all stopped.

If I were dead then there should have been no awareness. In the stopping of sensation there should have been nothing. Why was I still aware? It was wrong. It occurred to me that I might have just been knocked out. Surely that was the explanation.

I stood up to see my car knocked askew with many other cars pulled to the side of the road. I thought I should let them know I was all right. I looked down at my arms certain that they would be bloody, but they weren't. I touched my jaw, which took a nasty impact when I hit the pavement.

Again, nothing.

I turned to my place of final resting after the truck hit me, only to see a blanket covering a pile of something.

Was the something ---- me?

Yes it was.

I shouldn't be seeing this! I should be dead with no awareness or feeling.

It was wrong!

This type of experience was for the weak who dreamed of continuance.

I sat for a long time, long after they cleared the mess that was left by the incident. None of this agreed with my beliefs. I should be past all this.

Now what will I do?

The time passing does not register with me as before. I feel like I just arrived, but also here forever. There are others of whom I cannot quite see, but I know they are there. I am still trying to accept what has occurred. The sounds become whispers, maybe that is progress. I find myself curious for the next step.

The other side, now my side, has become interesting.

****

37

I Heard You

Dear Friend,

I could hear your voice over the hum of the machine that I could not identify at first. There was a long dark hallway from which I emerged into your dialogue. At first the tone soothed my sore head like a cool cloth. Gradually the words stopped jumbling and your message came loud, clear, and loving.

"Come back."

The wavering of emotion making me want to cry as well.

But I couldn't.

For some reason there was nothing in this poor body able to respond in any way. My thoughts sped along with all the muster I used to have throughout. What was wrong with me? I wanted to shout it as loud as I could. My hand to squeeze yours, but my fingers elusive to my senses.

I knew the body was there but it had no existence nor substance. The only thing keeping me sane was your voice. It centered my focus, letting me know I was not lost.

There was confusion while sleeping, for the dreams were so

lucid that I supposed that this was the dream, and that the reality. The joy of review dimming as I realized that indeed it was an illusion created by my mind.

"Come back to me."

I heard you.

I did.

However, the ability to move this inert force impossible. The path that led me to this situation materializing before me as I lay here. A car, a curb, a moment of distraction followed by a blow to my side and scrape of my cheek as my face met the pavement. I remember telling myself that I would look like hell with my hamburger face. I could feel a bit of gravel in my right eye. Its irritation keeping me focused for a brief while as I heard the chorus of voices crying for help.

After those first moments I floated between pain and a blurry comfort of drug induced euphoria. My body an amusement. My panic dulled, it was quite all right to just be there and wait. The calmness enveloped me and I remember nothing else.

I know I hovered between staying and going for what seemed like forever. In doing so I realized that no matter how this turned out, I still have forever, just not how I considered it.

I feel your beckoning and I want to respond. This body however is waning. There is not enough energy to bring it back.

I also know of your finite view of life. I struggled to give you a sign.

But I couldn't.

The only thing I can leave you is my thoughts. They create already in the next moment of our togetherness.

I feel your hand holding mine. Wet with your tears, I wish it could lift up to caress your face while giving you insight that this is not the end.

As I lift up out of the stillness I finally can see you as you keep vigil at my side. The fatigue that surrounds your form alarms me.

Drifting towards you I try to comfort you but it is evident that it falls on deaf ears.

The most curious thing is the body that lays so still on the bed.

"Is that me?"

I wonder.

The features are familiar but without my spirit, not so recognizable.

Brushing your cheek with my lips I realize I indeed must go. The return no longer feasible. It will not be repaired.

Know that I heard you well, the words comforting. I would have returned if the body could have continued.

Thank you for your kindness, love, and energy.

****

38

My Dad Arrived About An Hour Later

Dear Friend,

I turned my head literally leaving my body behind without so much as a thought. There was no indication it would fail so miserably or so quickly.

There was no pain, thus my confusion to find myself gazing back upon it while still feeling quite whole.

I sat on a nearby ledge waiting for someone to come by. In the early hours a short cut through the park, a popular path. It provided me with my daily meditation on the way to work. The days easier to cope with after communing with the trees. Certainly someone would be by soon.

I stared at myself sprawled upon the gravel path wondering if I could move it to a more sedate position. It was impossible to get close to it. A sort of barrier forming as the amount of time increased. So I sat there waiting until someone called an ambulance. Knowing it was “too late”, I reluctantly followed along not sure of how to deal with it all.

No one seemed to feel me or see me. It was like I had become nonexistent to everyone. That too, caused me some anxiousness but deep inside there was also a feeling of balance.

All this time so entranced was I with the process I did not think of the consequence upon my family. The feeling that this was all a dream prevailed. A hope of waking up in my bed still lingering. A bad dream hardly noteworthy to those of whom you love.

The doctors declaring me dead sent my head reeling. Surely it was time to wake up. They all walked away leaving me to stand alone with my self. What was I to do now?

The sounds of an emergency room distant in my thoughts with nowhere to go, I sat on a chair next to the body. It was not "me" any more, whatever had happened, the personality, awareness, and "being" of myself had transfixed to this state.

My dad arrived about an hour later. I stood up expecting to shake his hand but he passed by with his eyes upon the bed. Thankfully they had not removed me to the morgue. This was a kinder atmosphere for him to see me. His shoulders slumped when the sheet was lowered. I would have given anything in that moment to relieve his pain. He stood for a long time just looking at me.

I had been an only child. My mother had long since passed, so I knew this had great impact. This was the last connection he had with her physically. The child they had raised together now gone.

My hand felt warm upon his shoulder. I, in my ignorance thought he might detect me. The concentration of energy certainly building. All I wanted to do was let him know that I was there. In my desperation I leaned forward hoping, hoping. hoping.

After awhile he spoke out loud, his eyes looking towards the sky. I presumed he was searching for heaven, but this is what he said.

"I hope you are taking care of him, Rose. Keep the home fires burning until I get there."

Rose was the name of my mother. She had passed from cancer

several years before. My father had never gotten over it. He rarely spoke her name, claiming it was far too painful. Now here he was asking her to take care of me. The sweetness of his tone causing me to tear up.

I missed her too but I never expected to hear her voice so prominently.

“I promise I will keep him with me” said a familiar voice from behind.

I spun around to see her looking the same as she always had. Her smile caressing me while she extended the arms I knew so well.

“I knew you would Rose” said my father as he left the room.

Speechless in my mother’s arms, I felt the air around me beginning to stir. A feeling of acceleration enveloping us, we seemed to travel forward.

To where, did not seem to matter.

“We can be wherever we like until he gets here” she said. When he does we will adjust the plans.

It all felt right so I accepted the invitation. We wait for him still.

****

39

This Process Is A Subtle One

Dear Friend,

Since our last encounter a series of events has precipitated a change in my life. Our mutual respect and friendship lingers wistfully as I make my way from the world we shared.

Accordingly the first item of business begins with that last breath. There was not a hint of premonition as I expected. Always a gentleman with a spiritual point of view, my disappointment was great that I was caught so unaware.

My relationship with my god not as intimate as I thought. A slight stab of discomfort to the frontal lobe dropped me to the floor with a resounding thud. Embarrassment followed by panic filled me immediately. All hopes for a speedy recovery gone once the realization that motor skills were no longer functional.

Shouts of men echoing while a lone siren wailed off in the distance. Hurry! I thought clutching my body greedily with my soul. This process is a subtle one though the heartbeat deafening in its retreat.

A lady placing a sweater beneath my cheek while the feet of many crossed my line of vision. A cold nose of a Spaniel inspecting my inert hand. Unable to move it, I welcome the contact as it gives me hope.

A rush of men breaking through a morbid audience waiting to see if I will die. Some already turning away mentally noting my ashen skin tone.

"Already done for."

"Heart attack, poor guy."

"Did you see his eyes?"

All phases from a funeral beginning to take shape while I lay upon the pavement. The coldness overtaking the structure of life. A blanket wrapped tightly while a door slam alerts my senses to reality. A hover between is where my focus lies. Is there a choice or not?

A hum of a motor as the sigh of a siren makes yet another path to safety. I find astonishment in their belief that I am unable to hear them.

"Cardiac Arrest?"

"No. Aneurysm."

"Prognosis?"

"He's a goner."

The term, a primitive one showing a lack of education let alone sensitivity. My desire to bolt upright a huge one. Mustering my best, the best attainable movement comes from my right hand. The fact that it goes unnoticed is not lost upon me.

A "goner" it is then I whisper to myself. A droning buzz from a monitor confirms it. I am gone. If that is so, then where have I gone? At the insistence of my ego I find it a mission occupying my focus indefinitely.

The surroundings the same, melting into different scenarios upon my thoughts. Fascinating how it is in such harmony, never noticed it to be so pronounced before. There is no exact point of reference, only what creates itself from my desires.

The reenactment of the aneurysm replayed ad nauseum while I researched the process. We truly are products of our thoughts. The question arising as to where these thoughts originate if I haven't a brain to produce them.

It has since that initial question become apparent that it wasn't the body producing the thoughts after all. The soul. My soul is the source. Fascinating.

Inevitably a conclusion will come forth. I await with confidence. A note of solace not necessary. Feel sorry, not. I am well. Only in the process will there be any growth. Your friendship remains with me as I hope mine does for you. Until we come through the thoughts again. I will keep you close to my heart.

Unbelievably my heart does beat. I can hear it.

****

40

Realizing That During My Nap I Had Indeed Moved On

Dear Friend,

I woke up today with wonder, the pain had all but gone away. This was fantastic news seeing as how the previous days had been wrought with discomfort.

My first thoughts were to call my husband if this meant anything. I could be home for Thanksgiving. Whatever they were giving me was working. It was obvious.

I could see the parking lot from my bed if I sat as straight as I could. I wanted to know when Brad was coming so I could be fixed up. The buzzer to the nurse station was almost within reach. If I saw his arrival then I could get my purse for a little makeup. It had been so long since I had felt well that I wanted to look good as well.

I had been sick, for such a long time that the idea of this wore me out. I slipped into a light sleep as the hospital hummed around me. The constant vibration of activity never allowing full rest to come to me.

I had always been afraid I would die in here away from my family and friends. There could not be a worse scenario for me as

I lay in this bed. My fervent wish was to go home where I belonged. I hated the moment left to my own devices. The treatments were painful. I could feel myself weakening but was powerless to do anything about it. I need to get well.

I remember Brad telling me he would be back later. There were things with the children to tend to. Did I understand? Of course I did, they were my children as well. The memories of tending to them quite etched in my memory. Sure I could wait until he returned. I could use a nap anyway. The treatment today was a tough one. A nap sounded perfect. I could be awake when he returned. We could watch a movie or something.

Sure. I could tell he just wanted to get away for a brief moment of his own. All this hospital stuff was wearing him down. Yeah. I understood. If I could take a break I'd take one too.

Now I gazed out to the parking lot awaiting his return. I just wanted him to get here. His surprise at my strength would be such a boost.

But he did not arrive.

No one did.

Alone I waited realizing that during my nap I had indeed moved on to something better. Those I waited for would not come, but those who had known me always were there. Waiting until I was ready to accept the truth. Physical no longer in my path, at least not for now.

Funny how it all suddenly reveals itself to you. I thought there would be tears but there were not. I thought there would be fanfare of some sort, but all there was was a blink of an eye.

A nap that ended more than a drama, or was it? I am all right. I see Brand and now I wait for him.

****

41

It Is Important That You Know

Dear Friend,

I know full well how much you miss my presence. The touch of flesh accompanied by your eyes in mine..... a loss that's difficult to get over.

Know that I am able to perceive all of the daily actions participated by yourself. Though you cannot feel the touch of my hand I still connect. It is important that you understand that I thrive only in a different manner.

Crossing the distance between physical and spiritual not all that uncomfortable. In fact the event expanding what I considered to be me. A breath released causing the finality of the body actually an easy moment. It was not the moment of panic that I had always feared.

If I could I would wipe your tears gently instead of watching you wipe your own in sorrow. I am not gone from you. The relationship continues. Attempt to believe in the old physical chemistry we shared as it moves on.

Yes, we will have to be patient while our energies realign to accommodate the new situation. We can bemoan the perceived separation or we can readjust while awaiting the final eternal reunion.

Close your eyes while reliving our physical closeness. The mind is a powerful reenactment device that could quiet the current life pattern rather than to try to dissect it spiritually. As it would be virtually impossible.

We watch you lovingly waiting for an opportunity to assist you on the way. Our gaze coming in nonlinear terms as to not disturb you on your journey. This singular state does not do your energy justice. Our view of many levels blends and separates the energy strands simultaneously. You are much more.

In your heart we know there are glimpses of the big picture. A moment or two where you feel at one with the universe. In these moments it is important to identify yourself. Forget if you can the timeline that underlines your life line. Please note that the timeline, is one of many and has no bearing on your full entity existence. It is merely a tool to guide you in unfamiliar territory….. the physical plane. It is unfortunate that all of you become so attached to it.

So.

If you are able.

Transcend the timeline to no time when you are able. We are proud of your progress but wish complete fulfillment for you. Keep creating….. it's the only way.

****

42

So This Is God

Dear Friend,

I faintly recall my hands shaking when asked if I was Ok.

I was.

I really was.

The warmth came up my arm like a smooth piece of satin brushing the skin.

I rested my head on the headboard giggling furiously when it clunked just a little too hard. No one heard me though because they were off to other places of worship.

At least it looked that way. As for me the small room just expanded to another galaxy where I could fly.

I liked that.

It was better than this dump, that much made sense to me. During this blast to my mind I had a definite feeling of godliness. Like a peephole to heaven. That's what it was.

I had been on a quest to find the creator, you, the guy called god. I wanted to talk to him about the raw deal I had got when I was born here. Seems to me that the circumstances could have been more fortuitous or whatever that word for better is.

A long list of grievances filled me while the solace of heroin eased the rough edges. This was my ticket to salvation.

It was.

It was until….

…..I couldn't get back.

The man asking if I was okay became louder but I translated it to a whisper and ignored it. Where was this son of a bitch god? Why didn't he respond to my inquiries. He was to blame for this rotten excuse for a life.

What was the purpose of this suffering?

The warm blanket filled me.

How do I get an audience with god?

A room appears with a small table. An old man sits writing quietly and deliberately.

I demand to see god with all the hostility I can muster.

Where is this supreme loving guy?

The man at the table points to a door.

"God awaits you there" he said casting his eyes downward.

"Coward" I uttered walking away.

The door is heavy and hurts my arm. Inside is more of the same, another disrupting endeavor by this so called God.

I wait.

Only to see my reflection.

So this is god.

Me.

****

43

Someone Should Have Told Me About This I Thought

Dear Friend,

It may sound weird but I am almost heavenly. Without the body I be anywhere I want. It's beyond what I reckoned it would be.

I never thought much about the whole bit of death. Just assumed it would come when it would come just naturally. It did not knock on my door till I was old and ready. Maybe my attitude would have been different if it had happened when I was younger.

So it was that all of me just wore out. I kept waiting for disease, something that would be certain to finish one off. It never came. It just kept beating my old heart until it couldn't anymore.

It had started to snow that last day. Winter always my favorite seasonal experience. I was glad I got to see it one more time. Yea I knew, if that's what you are asking. It came up on me while I was washing some fruit in the sink. The flakes had begun to float down just like I remember as a child. The design they made upon my window pane gave me a moments pause as I watched it.

Suddenly I was young again. The room reminiscent of the home I lived in with my parents. The flakes came fast and furious. I thought about snowmen, something that had not occurred to me for years.

I looked down at my hands they were as smooth as a baby's bottom. The knuckles small not swollen from arthritis.

The smell of vanilla cookies filled my nostrils. The taste very close to my mouth. I was positively convinced that my mother would walk through the door at any second.

So lost in thought.

The memories becoming fluid enough to confuse my present.

I joyfully sat myself on the floor totally immersed in the vision. The rush of vitality long forgotten inciting my excitement at being young again.

The floor cold against my arms I moved slowly to the rug. A reprieve from discomfort immediate, the rush of spirit escaping this old body in constant motion. The leaving much quicker than I anticipated.

The snowflakes dancing just within my line of vision distracting my focus momentarily. Then suddenly the process complete. I look back upon it without remorse. It's weird but somehow natural. I never would have considered it so easy. Someone should have told me about this I thought.

Someone should have.

Everything not as they said.

Quite confusing, but now that I have passed I feel better.

Heavenly is a great description but so far not pearly gates. I guess that was a figment of someone's vivid imagination. If I run across them I will record my feelings if it's available. Now I move forward the destination open, the past behind me.

It's alright.

There's no pain just inquisitiveness.

I go happily.

****

44

I Am Still Here
I Am Right Next To You

Dear Friend,

I feel your energy pulling me. Your loneliness a cocoon of separation unbearable to you in so many ways. If there were a way to reverse the situation I would. My experience was cut short so unexpectedly. Life such a brief gift the ending of it always a surprise. Never was there a moment when it was intentional for me to be separated from you. Know this, the separation is only brought about by different vibrations. I am still here only my energy is different.

No longer is there the need for a physical body. Existence on a different level is all. I am right next to you, not like before. I feel your pain. My arms are around you while the tears run down your cheeks. My face reflects back to me in them. There are no words of comfort that reach your ears. My whispers bounce back to me and the realization that you have not heard me comes into my thoughts. These past months have been spent attempting different methods of communication.

As I stand here next to you the daily routine of your life gives me strength. Admiration fills me as the actions of your soul push forward with projected ideas. Not many are aware of your despair. None know of your broken heart while you smile and state that you are getting by. Only in the night when you call my name desperate for a sign. My hands brush your cheek. Focus so necessary for the action to occur. I am getting better at it but not quickly enough to end your loneliness.

Open your mind if you can to the possibility of a connection. I know you believe you have but the focus of your energy needs to be more accessible on many levels. Your sadness gets in the way as it closes around you like a cloak. The desperate attempt of myself thwarted by the wall it creates.

The right method still eludes me. This opportunity of the moment brief as I write this note. Please know I have not left. The attempts by myself will not ease. You are not alone. A way will be found. This is my promise to you my love.

****

45

Oh Lord I Be Dead

Dear Friend,

What be wrong with me? My arm don't work no more and my ears be ringing like church bells. I was supposed to be getting my chores dun fore sunset and here I be doing nothing. No one comes by this way to see me here in the brush. Well no one ever be getting me home. My Louisa be fixin some supper about now.

She be worrisome if I be late. I feel my heart, it beating something fierce. Still be frozen solid. There in the ground. I can see the curve in the road but nothing else. Am I dying? Sure be wishing I had gone to church this past Sunday. Louisa always getting on me about god and all.

If I die she be never be letting me hear the end of it. Here I is laughing in the brush about Louisa ratherin at me bout church. I think I might be meetin god pretty quick. Now I suppose church might be so good.

Oh my Lord my breath just got real hard to catch. I feel tears in my eyes. Don't wanna die, no sir. Maybe if I crawl I can get home so I don't die in the road like an animal. Sure would like to see Louisa about now.

I be feelin real scared. My Pa died in the road alone by the barn. Me found him in the straw lookin up at the sky. Always wondered what he be seeing. I look around but there's nothing to see. Maybe if I looked at the sky there will be those angels Preacher John always be talkin about. Maybe angels are what pa saw. Never could find out for certain him being dead and all. His face looking happy though. Still wonder what he saw.

There.

I roll over to see the sky. The sun dropping down behind the mountain. Crickets in my ears. It be sounding like a regular evening. Tomorrow there is more planting to do.

Oh my heart really hurts. I try stop the pain but it keep coming. Wish Louisa was here. The rings in my head getting louder. The sky now dark, stars shining. I wonder if I will see sunshine again.

No matter I suppose. Maybe there will be a sun in heaven. Preacher always talkin about lights in heaven.

The pain so bad I be wishin to die. Just when things be lookin real low I hear a voice. Praise God. I am found. Don't be knowing the fellow, new to these parts. I imagine I ask him to take me to Louisa. He helps me up and carries me on his back. As he be walkin every step I be feeling better. Right soon he puts me down and we be walking home. An invite to Louisa's cooking right on the tip of my tongue.

"What be your name" I ask.

The smile odd because the teeth are so white. Never seen teeth so white. Wondering where the man come from. Teeth like that just ain't natural.

No never mind though he dun take me home to Louisa. Things be allright now.

The door to the cabin wide open. Lots of people..... some I

know…. Others not. Odd. Louisa not telling me about guests. There be a man laying on the table. All dressed up in Sunday Church clothes. Now who would do a fool thing like that. Always curious I walk right up, my eyes not believing what they see.

It be me!

Oh Lord. I be dead.

I turn in a panic and run head on into the man with the white teeth. His arms around me while a shudder of fear goes through me.

"Its allright you know. You still exist." he says.

Sounds like he be schooled at least through a high grade. His hands on my shoulders I be feeling better. I just want to see Louisa one more time. Where she be?

Turning I see her sitting in the kitchen, her favorite spot in the world. Her eyes puffed out from carrying on I reckon. My hand on her shoulder she be lookin right at me.

I will not leave her. I be waiting right here till it's her time. My friend with the white teeth reckoned that be okay. He say he coming back for us both real soon.

It's all gonna be fine I just know it.

****

Note: The spelling in this message is exactly as it was written. Also this written message contained a mix of both long hand writing and printing.

46
I Hear My Name

Dear Friend,

My head swirls like a whirlpool. I am unable to find any sort of balance at all. What is the malady that plagues myself?

Where am I?

The struggle to reconstruct the event tires me. The more I labour the more frustration that builds inside my being.

My memory blurs at the mention of family. Surely I had one. In the peripheral eyeline I sense someone beside me.

What are they doing? Again, the focus necessary escapes me and I am left to wonder what is becoming of me.

A brief moment of rest feels good. No thoughts to tire the mind. Adrift on a raft of my own creation I feel myself rocking on waves of water like substance. The moment disrupted by the sound of voices. They appear to be increasing in volume. Are they calling my name? If so, who are they and what is their purpose?

My eyes are so heavy, the waves wrap around me like a cocoon. The thought of severe pain meets me and I retreat back to the cocoon.

There is a long moment of repose. In hopes that the calling

ceases I turn over and bury my head deeper in my place of comfort. If I do not do so I now know the pain would overwhelm me and either destroy me or drive me to madness.

A deep slumber envelopes me again. I am glad because the voices still call me. There is a thought that I might recognize the tone but I dismiss it all out of hand.

My eyes twitch and I feel the sensation of light upon them. The struggle to open my eyelids takes much concentration. The blinding light confuses me and I shut them to block out, not only the voices but blocking the pain would be a blessing.

I hear my name but am not sure from where. One voice is familiar but no identification comes to mind.

The situation continues. Where am I? My head feels heavy. Someone is holding my hand. My name again, a plea for deliverance. Deliverance to where? Confused I attempt to open my eyes. The light now dim defines an outline of a man. Oh yes, my husband, Dean. I smile and close my eyes. He squeezes my hand and I know where to drift to. The voices now a distant thought. I move forward to a place of comfort. The hope of Dean's arrival gives me peace. He will join me soon. I feel his hand letting go. I take it as a symbol to do the same.

I am free.

****

47

Was He Going To Rape Me?

Dear Friend,

The idea of death was the last thing on my mind when I left home that morning. I was filled with ideas of how my future was going to turn out. College days were almost behind me. My boyfriend Patrick had proposed marriage so now all that was left was getting a job.

With my keys in hand my thoughts were not focused on my surroundings. In retrospect I should have paid more attention. I should have seen it coming. However I was young, in love and so briskly on my way to the future.

It was the swiftness of the abduction that left me breathless. No sooner than I arrived at my car a hand covered my mouth.

Someone dragged me into the trunk of a car before a sound could be uttered. One would think that panicked thoughts would prompt me to try to escape. I did actually try but my pounding fell upon deaf ears of traffic noise. Several quick turns slammed me into the metal sides of the trunk. Bruised and confused I had no idea what the end of the tale would be.

I wondered who would do this. Would they rape? I could tell my abductor was a man, so while we raced through the streets my heart pounded in fear. Never once through did I anticipate death.

The car stopped abruptly causing a lot of dust to filter through. The coughing from it racked my already depleted body. My throat was parched with my mind creating a cold bottle of water.

The bright sun blinded me as I was jerked from the car. The man was almost shorter than I with a foul body odor. Was he going to rape me? I would have given him the whole seven dollars in my pocket just to let me go home. I debated whether to look at him or not. This judgement call was colored by all the crime shows I had watched over the years. If I could identify him he might have to kill me. Therefore I squinted my eyes closed feeling a drip of sweat roll into my left eye. Or maybe it was a tear. I'm not sure now.

Whoever he was, he stretched some sort of tape over my mouth. It stuck to my hair pulling it unmercifully as I pushed forward. Nary a sound came from my rough captor. I wanted to ask him who he was and why he had taken me from my life full of promise. What did I ever do to you I asked silently. His hot breath was on my neck as he pulled me into a secluded area. I recited to my self a prayer of endurance because I could already feel myself being assaulted. A rationalization of survival made the surreal events unfold easily in my thoughts. I awaited the attack but it did not occur as I thought.

The smell of cigarettes and sweat mingled with a hint of mint reminded me of a childhood event. At that time I had encountered a family relative who smelled like that. I kept waiting for the attack. When it came the force was so powerful it left little time for contemplation or fear.

His hands slipped around my neck crushing my wind pipe with one grasp. The shock of no air exploded in my temples while I struggled in vain to make him stop. I was unable to do so. My lungs burned with the over exertion in its quest for air. In defeat I lifted out of my body to safety. The rag doll form in his hands no longer needed for my existence. I wasn't afraid. I opened my eyes as the threat of reprisal for identification was no longer an issue.

I felt no pain or burning like I did when it began. The lifting out stopped all of that. The wondering did linger as to why he came after me.

Looking down at him closely I couldn't place where I might have encountered him before. Did that make me a random senseless victim?

The idea of that was more disturbing than the event itself. As I lifted out more thought expanded in my perceptions. Although this man was currently not placeable to me his trace soul was.

Pictures of another time came forth where the path was somewhat revised. The idea of balance kept ringing in my ears as I sailed forward. Funny how everything looks different when you view the whole picture. Our meeting merely an ending to a whole train of incidents.

I no longer feel any discomfort. The sadness of lost opportunity with Patrick fills me. However from my new perspective I see our paths crossing again.

I feel more energy as I drift away from my now dead body. This man leaving me having fulfilled a destiny that was not clear to him. I bear him no ill will. The balance now complete I await another rendezvous with time.

****

48

The Night I Died Was Tragic In That Moment

Dear Friend,

The night I died was tragic in that moment. It was not as if there wasn't any warning. The cancer cells had long inhabited my body. We were like old enemies doing a choreographed battle to the death. Of course I fought bitterly to the end. My belief system did not make room for an after life. Sure, all the stories of heaven and hell were presented but they never felt more than a child's bedtime story. I never felt the presence of anything other than myself and the world I lived it.

So on that last night there was a deep melancholy inside me. The final moment filled with the fear of nothingness. My mind had a hard time understanding that I was soon to be no more.

My family around me as well as a barrage of high tech equipment designated to keep me alive I caught a glimpse of myself in the window. Who ever was lying in that bed did not closely resemble me at all. This guy was worn from the battle. His eyes sunk in his head so far he looked ghastly. Where was the guy I remembered as myself. It would be nice to see him again. He was still there in my mind any ways.

I kept becoming weaker. The panic of loss covering me until I wept out of control. Where was the fairness in this? I did not want to die. I did not want to leave my family. I clenched my fists trying to muster up the energy to survive. I just couldn't do it.

Exhausted I turned my head into the pillow. I was so afraid of the final moment. Surely it would be painful and panic ridden. My heart began to race. My wife held my hand tightly. A small moan escaped my lips as I tried to hang on. I couldn't feel my body go limp as each organ stopped moving. It occurred to me that this was the final blow because I was still conscious. How cruel to be left with nothing and still be aware. It was worse than I could have imagined. I closed my eyes waiting for the final moment of consciousness.

Nothing happened.

My thought process continued. My body not functioning but mind going rapidly forward.

What was going on?

I opened my eyes and the scenario was the same. Family members crying. My wife with her head buried in the bedside.

Why were they so upset?

I actually felt better than I had in quite awhile. I sat up to tell them all so. Then it dawned on me. In those past moments I had died. I looked behind me and there I was. The poor body that was mine looked like a stranger. Without me in it there was no recognition for me. I remember hovering there for quite a while yes I said hovering.

It was all so bizarre. My first reaction was to console my wife but she couldn't hear me. So I just sat with my arm around her.

So now what?

The room began to waver in my vision. I heard voices but from some where else.

Now looking at it I see the process. Reality as I knew it faded away. It was still there but now I had a different perspective. All the voices gave way to the others. They included guides and old friends.

Ok.

So I was wrong.

I just wasn't paying enough attention. I thought it was important enough for me to let you all know.

There is more. . . . .

****

49

Before Birth There Were Many Plans Made

Dear Friend,

Inside my head exists a kaleidoscope of color. It splits into rainbow slivers and becomes a reality for my viewing. I have not participated in the way that I hoped. Before birth there were many plans made that never reached fruition. The disappointment felt receded after a time and there was renewal in the fact that I could at least breathe.

Perception is such a unique process. One can observe it while non physical but it doesn't hit home until you are solitary in a body. I remember the first moment of clarity. It was when I was one year and I realized I had indeed become a physical entity. Just the knowledge fed my spirit and I had evolved. It was in the next moment it became clear that something was not quite correct. Was it my failure or the failure of the universe I encountered. The doctors who were administering advice called it cerebral polyp.

I called it a plan gone awry. It was not what I envisioned and there was confusion as to my creative abilities as to what went wrong.

When I was there I saw my parents struggle together in my developmental process. The guilt was an enigma to me. It was not what I planned. It had been my hope to draw them together and that my birth would give them satisfaction and a reason for existence. All that transpired was two parents sick with worry about a child whose future seemed dim.

I was a multidimensional being. How could it be that I was this dependent physical form with no creative abilities at all. What happened to mis align my spiritual self with what?

As I progressed in this life there was always the underlying question of why? Why would I choose to do this to myself and my parents. Surely I was a victim of circumstance.

This was not what I was expecting. By the time I was eighteen my parents still had to take care of me. They worked together in harmony by this time. Issues that had been at the surface when I was eight had receded to the depths of their unconscious. They were indeed in harmony.

On a Sunday afternoon they had taken me for a ride. The choice was to the mountains for brunch at a ski resort. They wanted me to see snow for the first time. We were all excited.

The last curve before the summit twisted in an odd angle. We all went over the cliff before we could take a breath.

The plummet was in slow motion. The view went beyond the physical making a revelation.

My disability, a necessary aid in their growth. My disability a necessary hinderance to my arrogance.

Justified. Suitable.

Thank god it all occurred.

We move forward.

****

50

Where Am I? I Ask

Dear Friend,

My eyes grow heavy as I keep walking. A moment of rest outside my grasp. It seems I have been moving toward something my entire life. Always in the peripheral always gone when I direct full attention.

As the journey continues I struggle to remember that prequel. How did I get here and why am I so tired? There were plans to rest before continuing of this I am most certain.

The path blurs at the edges while my confusion multiplies. What to remember escapes me at every turn. All there is, is the path. I keep walking. Certainly there will be a final destination.

I turn my head into remembrance of what still remains unknown. As the walk continues there are great strides in my attempt to remember. Blurred images stand at my side. The focus still just beyond my fingertips. My eyes close with relief as I feel the softness of something against my cheek. Someone has had pity while embracing my weariness.

Still walking the path becomes more distinct. There is a gravel line that was not there before. Is it progress or delusion. Still so tired. I look beyond my regular line of vision. I find myself startled to see my mother. What does her presence mean on my path.

I struggle to remember that last time I saw my mom. Her profile moving forward in my memory. She drove away from me when I was thirteen. Just beginning junior high school a young girl needs her mother. I see her with a printed scarf on her head turning the corner in her chevy. She drove soon after into an oncoming tractor trailer at the corner of Maple and Third. Never did I see her again after that morning, only to see her now waving at me from across the street. My peripheral vision becoming more specific. Turning towards her I see that she still looks the same. A scarf covers her brunette hair in the same manner it did so long ago in Jr. High. My first inclination is to scold her for being away so long. Didn't she know how much I needed her at thirteen? However, I keep walking, taking her image with me. She touches my hand. I forgive her.

For all the first dates she missed, the wedding she never witnessed. Her smile warming some bitterness that clung to me somehow my whole adult life.

I am still not sure where the path goes but it's best to keep walking. I see my brother Samuel. He's so much older than I. Too bad we never had a relationship. By the time I was old enough he was too old. Missed each other by a breath of time. He falls into rhythm with me and we keep walking.

"Where are you going sis" he asks.

"I'm not sure." I reply.

"Why don't ya stop for a minute?" he said. The thought was intriguing but I was certain there was some place to go.

"You're already here." He said.

I feel myself becoming anxious but I cannot stop. If I stop there has to be a reckoning and I am not ready yet. It's fluid motion.

Definition causing my heart to pound. Indeed I am not ready.

Still ono the path I encounter a dog. Odd for such an occasion. Why a dog? It comes forward tongue wagging along with its tail. It seems vaguely familiar yet I struggle to remember the dog. He begins to walk with me without a leash. His pace in harmony with mine. Glancing down I remember wishing I had a dog when I was child. The acceptance of this canine and my process so important. I have never felt more in league with another life form. We turn the corner as the form changes to a woman. I remember that face but unable to place where. She turns to me while smiling. Then I remember.

A flat tire, a lonely road, a by passer in a red Volkswagen stopping and a pair of smiling eyes willing to lend a hand. Those eyes now reflect back on me while I tried to recall her name.

"Not necessary," she said.

"I just came by to help you again. Seems like you're always on a singular path, looking for help. I'm here. Just so you know."

With that she jogged ahead of me on the path. Yes I remember her. In fact those eyes had gazed back at me many times. Where? I am not certain.

I slow my pace. Images start to form showing me a crowd. Why can I not focus the way I want? The direction suddenly feels incorrect.

Looking to my right it alarms me to see that I have circled around ending up exactly where I started. I must have looped around unknowingly. The scenery coming into focus. I feel like it's a déjà vu. I used to have those when I was in my thirties. There was some scientific reason for them but it was fun to imagine some predetermined psyche phenomena attached to them. All of the surrounding are familiar. It's certain I have been here before.

My mother comes closer and I see the mole on her cheek that I use to gaze at when I was three. It would disappear in a laugh line while she giggled and played with my dolls and me. It still looks the same. Am I insane?

"No you're not!"

A voice from behind me. Turning I see a stranger, a young good looking man I can't place.

"Where am I?" I ask.

"You're home." Said a small voice from beside me. A young girl with eyes of green. A mischievous grin on her face she takes my hand and says

"Let's play!"

****

51

Gone Were The Physical Concerns

Dear Friend,

It is a puzzling state of affairs to find oneself looking at one's self. On first glance there is a double take that causes your heart to quicken. It is followed by denial. There must be some mistake you cry. This is not occurring. You watch the events unfold as they dispose of the body. The funeral, the grave yard, the burial all tumbling together as you watch it all seems helpless.

I wanted to scream "STOP" so many times I wanted to sit down with my mother. I wanted to go to my sewing class on Monday nights. I had been learning how to baste a hem only a few weeks ago. Surely I could still participate. I am still here.

The readjustment to non physical can be depressing. Actually I found it to be interesting. Gone were certain key prompts that usually sent me into a tizzy. Gone were physical concerns. The walking through walls part quite enjoyable. The lack of connection with those I loved quite psychologically destabilizing. All I wanted to do was talk to my mother.

Simple yes?

However after several attempts to get her attention failed I resorted to old fashioned haunting.

Laugh all you want. I remember feeling quite the same on all Hallows Eve. It used to be quite a joke. However this type of manifestation does somehow work.

I still want to measure time. I guess it is ingrained. The idea it does not exist fills me with anxiety. How long must I languish here. This place is surely not the final step.

I have connected with others in the same light. They all have elaborate stories of their passings to share. Most all pretty predictable while others shock the senses with their improbability. Now that I have stabilized I find the whole adventure quite intriguing. If I hold my thought clearly they seem to materialize in detail before my eyes. It seems familiar this process though not quite as easy then as it is now to produce.

I am quite pleased with my surroundings. Every detail the same as that which I thought previously. This manifestation a gift without knowing. I hope I can always know.

I am still perplexed by my lack of body. I can see fingers and toes but the solid part of me is lost somewhere in the translation to spirit. Spirit being harder to define with the limited perceptions I have still connected to the physical.

Does it have to be this confusing. Can I not just become spirit and be done with the physical, or do I have to balance for better knowing? I wish the answers were simple. Yet they are not.

It is terrible thing to feel alone. It is something I have avoided this entire past physical existence. Now that I found myself solitary I want to opt out in despair so that I can reunite myself with someone.

Anyone.

It is a singular path but a friend or two along the way often softens the blow of growth so that you may continue.

I feel better knowing that there is indeed more. I never quite reconciled myself that so while incarnated. Now I know better.

So I walk forward.

Alone yet unafraid.

The future already exists. I just have to walk into it.

So be it.

****

52

Cancer

Dear Friend,

The light from within was something I always thought of as myth. Religion classes are filled with such nonsense of which I never paid much attention to. My head always occupied with more tangible thoughts. You lived but once wild and wooly. Whatever came afterward not so important at least not to me. It severed me to have an abrupt and final ending with no cause for retribution. I came from nothing and would return to nothing. Plain and simple. To hope for more or to actually believe in more was way too complicated for my life style.

I grew to manhood it seemed very quickly. My twenties and thirties were filled with fast times and fast cars. And yes fast women. I never connected if I could help it. To do so would require a commitment to truth on my part. I wasn't into it. I just wanted to experience life as much as I could. Cause once your gone, you're gone baby. Over and out.

I pretty much clung to that philosophy through my forties. After that the denial thing set in. I became a student of fine health and took care of myself. It was all working out quite well. I would live as long as I could and then be ok with death. After all I had had one hell of a life.

Who needed an afterlife?

Well let me tell you.

At the age of sixty two the unimaginable happened. I got sick. It wasn't part of the plan. I was supposed to live until ninety or so. I went for a second opinion, then a third, and finally a fourth. All the answers were the same.

Cancer.

A word not in line with who I was. Not a word I ever thought I would even utter let alone be a part of.

I started on a strict regimen of what would determine chemical poisoning right after they removed what they could. I guess you can hold quite a bit of cancer in your colon. I never realized it was that large. For a guy so obsessed with the physical you'd think I would have been a bit more knowledgeable with biology.

My hair fell out. I lost weight. It seemed that my body was on a fast track to oblivion. Funny how you can become obsessed with living when it's about to be taken from you. It's also funny how suddenly you start to believe in an afterlife. I guess it's kind of out of necessity. I felt somewhat fraudulent in my turn around. The word death not palatable. The word spiritual suddenly tasting very good with each moment.

My friends felt sorry for me. Total strangers knew of my coming demise. It was written all over me I guess. Let me tell you there was a dramatic change in my perception. However the final moment still seemed way out there somewhere. I rallied in the spring. There was hope it was all behind me. The physical discomfort receded. I thought there would be more but I was ultimately wrong.

The end came on a winter afternoon. Wrapped in a blanket I just couldn't get warm. The treatments had ravaged my body more than the disease I think. To my dismay I was unable to lift my head to take a sip out of a glass. I could feel the energy draining and it alarmed me. Now the end of life was becoming a fearful place. Gone were my sarcastic remarks about eternal life. Gone were the days of my so called eternal physical existence. I now waited wondering what would indeed happen. Would I be swallowed up by a cosmic energy? Would there be pearly gate of heaven? Or, would there be as I always thought, a changing of a door and forever darkness of nothing, as I disappeared from life and the thought of the universe?

Would I be just dust?

I cried myself to sleep more than one night pondering these questions. My fear multiplying until it swallowed me up. The last day I curled up under my blanket with my eyes tightly closed. It was as if I was waiting for the final blow.

It never came.

I was too weak to go to bed that night so I stayed on the couch. The pills they gave me for the pain not working so well anymore. My friend Patsy had stopped by earlier offering to stay but I refused. I remember her lips as they brushed my cheek. She had said "Bon voyage my friend". The click of the door lock, a final salute as she left.

Holding my pillow to my chest I thought about dying, waiting for it to come. There was a rhythm to my body that wasn't there before. I concentrated on my breathing. In out. In out.

I must have dozed off early because I was awakened by the sound of a party from a gathering across the street. I got up to see what was happening. It appeared to be a family party. I used to love parties. Never missed an invitation if I could help it.

Without thinking I decided I felt better. I stood up and thought what the hell? I'll go to the party. It didn't matter that I didn't know anyone there. What did I care what anyone thought. I was going to be dead very soon. The it would be game over. Who would care if I crashed a party?

I went upstairs to change. It had been a long time since I had dressed up. Hopefully my clothes were still in style. Looking in the mirror I decided that I didn't look too bad for someone with terminal cancer. Pleased with myself I started out for the party.

Walking up the sidewalk I could hear laughter from within. It reminded me somehow of when I was in college going from one party to another on a Saturday night.

My heart actually started to beat faster. This was going to be exciting. I could use some excitement. I put my finger upon the doorknob.

Now I really didn't expect to know anyone. I thought I would crash it, get a few laughs then leave. Imagine my astonishment when the person who answered the door was my grandfather. He was in mid laugh as he swung the door open. He looked right at me and cried "Stephen my boy! Come in! We've been waiting for you."

We?

What was my grandfather doing here. Last time I saw him he was lying in a hospital bed. That was thirty years ago. He should be over one hundred years old by now. He looked the same, only healthy.

What was happening?

None of this makes sense. He invited me in and I realized I knew everyone at the party. There was my high school friend Sam who had died in a drunken car crash when he was seventeen. My mother stood in the corner with a martini. She had had a heart attack seven years ago.

They all turned to me and said a collective welcome. I was stunned. I put my hands over my eyes as I realized I felt pretty good. The pain was gone. What was going on?

A diminutive woman stepped forward. She took my hand and smiled.

“Welcome Stephen” she said.

So I stepped across the threshold while I crossed into my biggest fear.

Death.

It wasn’t what I expected.

Not at all.

The party continued.

I was in spirit.

Nothing to it.

Nothing at all.

****

53

I Know That I Am Dead

The darkness surrounds me. I am afraid. Beyond that which is me, there is a void unexplored by human eyes. This void is like a small room where I retreat upon sleep and ultimately death. The dream envelops me briefly but I realize there will be a time where it envelops me completely and there will be no return. It scares me but I find bravery in the moment. I proceed to my destiny while in a dream.

My eyes open as the mist of the unreal recedes while I focus upon a room. It is small but vast, filled with crystals of every shape and size. I enjoy their energy as I revel in their existence in this self imposed dream state. I know I am dead. I know the significance of the crystals. They are records of the patterns of my past existences. If I hold one to my non existent temple I can relive that particular life. The diary of my progression recorded so solemnly in these crystals allowing me to proceed to another level not known to me before. I am exuberant at this revelation. What a gift to review past projections to a level such as this. My respect for these receptacles has been minimal before this precise moment. A record of all that has transpired allows me to process my advancement. What a coup! A crystal holds the key to remembering. This room I am now manifesting my self is a record keeping receptacle of me! Please know whatever you are that these places exist for all. Yours is next to mine. This is why I am able to leave you this message. Your attraction is not unusual, there is purpose to it. There are so many lighted crystals around me. Some I recognize from my physical life. Some are new. They are holding everything I need to know. By holding them to my temple I am also able to remember past lessons.

Death has become a blur. Now I exist within the receptables of me. They are now surrounding me. They caress my soul and give me comfort. As they will you. . . . .

I am finished. I will attempt another moment with you at another time. The crystals are full of energy. We go now. The moment has drawn to a close.

Adieu.

****

54

When The Opportunity Arose To Be Your Child I Was Unable To Say No

I was with you but a brief moment. The measurement of time dims in my memory but I can recall the quantity of it. The quantity was small but completely exhilarating. I wanted to experience your touch once again. The smooth skin of your palm on my cheek is a memory I've carried from life to life. When the opportunity arose to be your child I was unable to say no. Now sensing your grief I feel perhaps that it was a selfish error. Your quiet also disturbs me. My demise was of my own lack of decision. The sights and sounds of physical life enveloped me from the first breath. I was intoxicated with the denseness of it all. Waiting to develop all of my senses was trying to say the least. The small bursts of temper you never understood was merely my frustration at all the physical limitations. The measurement of time was excruciatingly slow. When I was finally able to walk, it was no wonder I took off in such a haste. I wanted to feel the wind whistle by my ears. I wanted to taste the air as I was breathing. I wanted to look into the blue sky and immerse myself into the color.

I wanted to feel the grass press against my back. All these things I did feel when I ran from you that morning. In complete abandon without any caution I stepped in front of that bicycle. It should not have killed me but my skull had not completely developed so the damage was severe. It was however a moment of complete joy for me. I was able to consume the whole experience in an instant. My only regret is your sadness. Please do not feel badly. It was all in line with my growth. Know that by my lack of perception I was killed, not by anything you did or didn't do.

Know that I still exist and that you will see my essence again. Perhaps in a different format. I understand your isolation but you are choosing to put yourself there. This experience has benefited us both. I can't say I'll wait for you but know that our essences are drawn to each other. The magnetism will occur again. Know no guilt. It was my choice. Stand up and live this life you have taken.

It's the only way to reunion.

I love you.

****

55

I Didn't Plan On Dying It Just Happened

Dear Friend,

I spent my whole life looking for God. It was said he could be found in the faces of Children, the goodness of others and the Church. Of course these were only a few of the named locations of his whereabouts. I can assure you however I searched in all of them and he wasn't there. So I spent my life looking in my own special way. I never found him in the normal reality of the masses so I drank and drugged my way into his presence…… or so I thought I did. My life was a series of chemical and natural highs and lows. Each episode convincing myself that I was almost there. In the process I hated myself more and more. The radical behavior all but made me a social outcast. My claims of divine searching's scoffed at by those that I loved. Everyone tried to understand but could not take the erratic behavior induced by my quest.

So it was I died alone. I was actually sleeping on the floor of a friend's apartment. The guy was my new best friend and he was wired to the best stuff in town. I didn't plan on dying, it just happened. The redeeming factor was that now at last God had no place to hide.

I looked for a bright light. There wasn't one. I looked for a tunnel. There wasn't one. In fact I couldn't get out of this guy's apartment. There I was looking at myself dead on the floor. I looked like I was sleeping. I knew it was just a matter of time until this guy woke up and figured out I was a goner.

It seemed like forever but there was a sharp knock at the door. I figured this would wake up my friend. Maybe I would be released to continue my journey to God. The knocking continued but no one moved, maybe he was dead as well. I stepped lightly over him as I opened the door. Imagine my surprise to see a beautiful woman standing there. I thought since I was dead that none of this was really happening but I was wrong.

She looked me right in the eye as she walked in.

It turns out that her name is Regina. I asked all the typical dumb questions to which she confirmed that yes I was dead. I tried to tell her about my search for God. That so far no matter what I came up with I was wrong.

Imagine my shock when she replied that I had arrived in God's presence. Now I really thought this girl was great but obviously missing a few marbles. I had searched my whole life. Now it appeared I was going to search my whole death. All I wanted was out. Out of here, out of body and out of physical life.

Where was God if he was so real? Why did he hide? Better yet, what was he hiding?

Regina smiled (which was great by the way). She turned me to the wall mirror. "There he is" she said.

Regina had a sense of beauty. Now it appeared she also had a great sense of humor. Poor kid. She just didn't get it. Again she pointed at my reflection claiming I was God. He lived inside of me all the time. I was searching outside of me.

Of course I didn't believe her. She was young and beautiful but obviously not very spiritual. My search transcended her limited experience when it came to finding God.

Regina was not offended though. She understood if I wanted to continue my search that it was possible. Simply request a new vehicle since the one I had been using was no longer available. She escorted me to the door which had just opened. Looking out at the horizon I could see two people walking hand in hand. One was a woman who appeared pregnant. They already knew I was the one they were looking for.

I knew this felt right so I did as she asked. However this opportunity to write it appeared a brief moment before I took their hands. I looked back to Regina but she was gone.

In the distance I could hear singing. Being dead is most definitely bizarre. It sounded like a chorus. They were singing Ave Regina over and over. That's when it hit me. She was the mother of God according to the bible. My choice is already made but now I realize that she was right. I will live the next life differently.

Just thought someone would benefit from my story.

****

56

How Could This Be?

Dear Friend,

My head feels light as if I had spun about until I became dizzy. I tried this frequently as a child. Stopping abruptly I would watch my world wobble before me until my eyes caught up with the rotation. The sensation wells up inside me as I try to remember why I feel this way.

Everything about me is the same. My room looks untouched from this morning. All of my clothes scattered about the room exactly where I left them. The television has moved forward on its programming a lively talk show coming through the speakers. The last time I checked it was the midday news. Squinting my eyes I look for my clock. There it is on the floor. Looking closely I see it was now 5 pm. I must have fallen asleep. The afternoon slipped through my fingers unnoticed again.

It must have been the glass of wine I had at lunch. Not being used to alcohol at lunchtime. Must have knocked me out. I decided to wait a bit until my head stopped spinning.

The pillows smell of lavender my favorite scent. The crisp sheets draped over my legs feel silky. I should just bite the bullet and get up. I am sure if I get up I'll feel better.

It seems like a long time before I throw my legs over the side of the bed and sit up. It must be past six by now.

My head feels a bit more stable as I stumble to the bathroom. Not bothering to turn on the lights. I splash some cold water on my face. Reaching for a towel I knock a bottle of lotion onto the floor. Bending down to pick it up, I notice something peculiar. I cannot see the reflection in the mirror. Drying my face I look directly at what I think should be me. I see nothing immediately.

Certain that the twilight is playing tricks on me I reach for the light. It cascades through the room and again even in full light there is nothing.

Not wanting to become alarmed I wipe my face again then I wipe the mirror. It must have steamed up when I ran the water. Again nothing. The reality not quite registering in my light head.

Tuning on my heels I return to the bedroom. It had now become darker. I figured it must be after 8pm at least. Shadows from the street lights dance across the carpet towards the bed. I may as well get dressed and go downstairs. As I approach my dresser I look through the mirror. It reflects a body sleeping in my bed. A wave of alarm passes through me.

An intruder.

Perhaps even a rapist.

Slowly I turned to get a better look.

It did not appear threatening in that the figure almost looked child like. I slowly walked towards it in my mind peaked with curiosity. Who ever it was they were sound asleep. I couldn't for the life of me figure out who was sleeping in my bed. Reaching out I pulled back the covers. My eyes saw but my mind could not comprehend the sight before me.

There, lying perfectly still was me. I must have stood there for hours completely frozen in disbelief.

How could this be?

Sitting on the edge of the bed I held my own hand. Thoughts of why, how and where reeled through my mind. It wasn't possible. I even tried to wake myself up.

No luck.

Was I dead?

Feeling vulnerable I laid down beside myself. I lightly touched my cheek as if to reconnect life force back into it. Closing my eyes I decided to rest a bit until I could think more clearly. My head throbbed with anxiety.

Yes. Yes.

Just a little rest would be good. The pillows so soft beneath my head…..

…..My head feels light, almost as if I had spun about until I became dizzy. I did this frequently as a child. Stopping abruptly I would watch my room wobble before me until my eyes caught up with the rotation. The sensation wells up inside of me as I try to remember why I feel this way…..

****

57

A Good Lesson For A Wise Guy Like Me

Dear Friend,

What's a jerk like me doing in a place like this? The Pearly gates should be over there. St. Peter or some one like him taking names at the door. That's what my old lady told me at least. Sunday school stories never fell on my ears I tell ya. Always skipped out on those classes. There was something better brewing down on the corner for a guy like me. I got blasted a week or so ago by a punk from the Northside. Unloaded a couple of shots while driving by in an old Rambler. Caught me by surprise it did. I knew the business was risky but bullets from a Rambler was not in the cards.

At least they took me to a hospital and did not leave me laying in the middle of the street. Would have killed my ma to see that. The doc made an effort to stop the bleeding but no luck. I wasn't awake but I knew just the same….. there was no waking up for me. Funny, how once you own that every thing else has a way of working out.

Once the last breath left my body I looked around for some relatives or the like. A buddy of mine ran into some trouble last year at the liquor store. Got himself popped real good. Maybe he will be around to show me the ropes. There was also my grand pop who died of lung cancer when I was twelve. He always brought me Grape Nehi soda. I miss him still. The silence was deafening as I left my body. Where was the harp music with angels. Chuckling to myself at that one the sound of foot steps suddenly came into focus. Who was coming? Over my left shoulder there was a presence, it looked like a little girl. Didn't know any little girls though she looked familiar. Slowly she approached smiling right at me.

Who was she?

I was soon to find out.

The little girl embraced me, the smell of her hair triggering a memory from my childhood. I had had an aunt who passed away when I was a kid. She used to buy me little things like candy and baseball cards. If I looked deeply into this kid's eyes I could see the reflection of my aunt in them. Could it be her?

The answer it seemed that this was her favorite form and that when she interacted with me she had felt child like..... God!..... where was all this coming from. It was like being read a story.

I didn't want to spend time with an aunt who brought me candy. When I was a kid I wanted to find out other things like who was going to with the Kentucky Derby --- Just kidding!

Anyways this little girl comes up to me and says.....

"Why did you do it?"

Do what?" I don't recall anything I did to my aunt. What was going on here? Was she really my aunt or what.

Again she repeated "Why did you do it?"

I felt like this was some sort of heaven or hell. Choice. Maybe St. Peter was going to show up at the Pearly Gates after all.

Again she repeated "Why did you do it?"

At loss for an answer I simply ignored her. The thoughts running through my head it suddenly dawned on me. When I went back on the street I remember shooting off a few rounds. Out of the corner of my eye the image of a small girl hitting the sidewalk about the same time I hit the pavement. I shot her without meaning to. What did she want? Some sort of apology? Yeah right!

What difference would it make now. I was reckless okay.

What can I say?

Her eyes accusing me. My consciousness making me feel guilty.

"You've always been reckless" she said.

"Want to see the consequences of it?"

In that moment I did see St. Peter and the gates opened. There was everyone I ever loved along with everyone I screwed over.

Why did I do it?

Out of a lack of understanding how things unfold. You really do reap what you sow. A good lesson for a wise guy like me.

****

58

It Is Not What We Were Told It Would Be

Dear Friend,

It was the anger that did me in, not all the other stuff that bothered me. In retrospect none of it really made a difference in how my life was going. I thought it did but that only fed my victimhood. How much easier was it to cop to circumstances that I was actually responsible for. Even now my blood boils at the thought.

I've looked around this supposed place of rest. It is not what we were told it would be. There is no rest only more to understand and evolve towards. I guess it is allright but the anger still fills me. I don't get how to leave it behind, I just don't. Does that mean I will repeat it all next time? Well that doesn't feel right either.

Looking back to where I just came from I see it clearly lurking in every facet of my life. The action was not only anger, only an after thought.

So now what am I supposed to do with this? Reincarnate to fix it? Seems ridiculous to me. I should be able to do something about it from here.

When I ask who designed this cockamamie process there is no

one to answer me. There are voices and a feeling of a Prescence but so far that is all. If I keep very still the voices say I need to let it go. I need to not be so angry. Well let me tell you I am angry at a lot of things. I guess especially at myself but that doesn't excuse all those who did me wrong. It's because of them that I am where I am today. Give me a few moments with them and I'll straighten this all out. Yes sir, I will!

Let it go, right.

Deal with myself, right.

The voices keep repeating they are with me. Well, where are they? My eyes close while the space around me changes. To what I don't know.

I realize it's all starting over again.

Life.

Great.

What is it about the process that I'm not getting.

My anger? Or the unfairness of a God who sees fit to torture me again.

Great.

Here I go.

.....It was the anger that did me in.....

****

59

The Death Process Begins While Living

Dear Friend,

I am torn in my decision of whether to stay or go. Your grip on my hand keeps the focus steady as the energy from my limbs is desperate. It's a funny feeling this dying. On one hand the release of discomfort and pain is welcome. The other gives a feeling of apprehension, the unknown as it unfolds.

The choice not made for you as one would think. The death process begins while living. Manifesting itself appropriately on the day you decide.

I understand if you disagree, it's much easier to play the victim in death. To believe the power of life is in someone else's hands is always more comfortable. However, from my current position I see the pattern. Death comes when you are ready or if you decide it's time.

Your hand in mine is soothing. It whispers your love and desire for me to stay. My body so ravaged by disease it seems most impossible. I feel the energy lift outside myself, the view much clearer here. To my right are those who await me, my mother, my father, my dog Scruff. To the other is my hand grounding itself in yours beseeching me to stay.

What do I do?

If one believes in the continuance of spirit then the reunion will take place in our hearts. This body hardly capable of functioning is tired. almost useless.

Let's make a pact to meet again when the blood flows ever more smoothly. You're right, we have so much more to do but this vehicle does not respond the way it used to.

The decision made when the disease took root I now succumb to its energy. My hand grows limp as the force recedes. Do not feel alone I still see you. Weep not for the shell that housed me. It disintegrates even now in this bed.

I feel your heart beat strongly, its rhythm rocking me to sleep. As always you comfort my spirit. Now my intent is to do the same.

Know we are connected.

Feel me.

Feel strong.

Feel love.

The body just a costume for who we all really are.

I feel no pain. Only the vastness which is my true identity.

****

60

My Name Was/Is Tim

Dear Friend,

I was always told that subconsciously a person knows when their time is up. Indeed there are many recorded examples of just such a thing. My thoughts throughout this past life were filled with questions about the signs. Were they obvious? Were they personal? Or did we just drop dead without a sign from anyone even ourselves? My patterns have always included a pursuit of the spiritual. My choices of exploration were filled with alternative studies. Not often condoned by the general population. My broad view or what I thought was a broad view was severely compromised on my own death. It was nothing like I thought it would be. Then again nothing ever is, is it?

Let me back up a bit on my story. My name was/is Tim. The state of Missouri was my home, until I went to college in Iowa. A real midwestern home bred kind of guy. No one you'd suspect of inner travels and nontraditional spiritual viewpoints. I played football, ran track, and did well on my academics. My whole future before me was an endless progression of opportunity. My girl friend was beautiful and she loved me. There was nothing but hope and promise to my life. In my communion with my guides there was never even a hint of demise. You would have thought there would be a clue of sorts. A moment of clarity that would have prepared me for what was to be.

The event occurred two months after graduation from Iowa State. I had gone home to Missouri to job hunt. My parents were thrilled to have me home for this short time. We were having a good time together. It was great to be their friend and enjoy the intimacy of family.

It was late one evening when I felt the odd sensation. My head felt light and there was a mild headache that had lingered with me most of the day. Assuming I was fighting "a bug" I went to my room after the news. I never made it to my bed. A searing pain started in my left eye. What occurred next was not in my scope of reality. My eyes clouded over and there were spasms on the left side of the body.

Trying to call out proved fruitless. The ground came up to meet me with great force. My face slammed into the carpet while my right arm tried desperately to cling to anything solid for stability. And there I layed until the next morning when my younger brother found me comatose on the floor.

The stay in the hospital was odd. Never regaining consciousness there was a struggle inside me to regain control of my now unusable body. What was going on here?

This was not how it was supposed to be. There was a parade of family and friends who tried to lead a pep squad of healing to me. All of them feeling awkward. Most of them reciting traditional prayers. None of them realizing that though my body was still there, the soul of my existence hovered in limbo. Not sure what to do next.

Would I get some guidance on this? Where were my guides?

I felt trapped and alone. My body still breathing technically but my essence acting like it was ready to go. Pretty screwed up if you asked me.

The seven day stay was highlighted by the anguish of my

parents when they were told I probably would not wake up. It was an aneurysm. I should have died instantly. My strong constitution forbade it. My parents were advised to pull the plug. Of course they couldn't do it. They were in complete denial always optimistic I would wake up.

So the wait began. I would sit and watch my lungs slowly respond to the respirator. The opportunities played out in my mind instead of the physical plane. There were some journeys but for some reason all the paths ended here.

Why wasn't I forewarned of this? I felt unjustly treated by an uncaring universe.

There were opportunities to communicate with my mother. She came everyday always in compliance with my father's wishes. She did not let me go. Her soul knew she should but she didn't.

Sitting next to her I attempted to comfort her. There was no suffering for me other than the fact I was stuck in between. Something or someone needed to let me go. I was not sure what the process was.

At the end of the seventh day my mother suddenly sat erect in her chair. Standing up she moved towards my lifeless form. My eyes felt like I was seeing things. She reached down and pulled the plug.

"There. Tim, now get on with it."

The moment overwhelmed me. It was suddenly clear what this was all about. Not what I thought at all. It was about my mother finding her strength to let me go.

I watched my lungs take their final breath. There was a release that pushed me forward through what seemed to be pillows of air. I arrived in a plane that seemed very familiar. It was what I had always imagined and more. Suddenly comforted it was obvious to me that sometimes death is a drama. Manifested for another's growth. Interesting. I now move forward to new adventure. The last incarnation and its end definitely having impact.

I wonder what will be next.

****

61

I Wish You Could Hear Me!

Dear Friend,

I watch you every day. Do you feel me? I sense your sadness at my departure. Your loneliness disturbs me. Your bitterness at the unfolding events hinders our contact at the new level. I wish fervently that it will dissipate with time.

Time.

How do I define it in my own present. The confusion draws me closer to your perception. Oddly this makes communication more viable. The newness of my situation becomes easier to deal with. Your adjustment to my withdrawal on equal footing with my adjustments in this frame of existence.

My desire for your acknowledgement paramount for me. I am here. Do you not see my message? The subtleness between dimensions obvious but difficult to transcend.

I am here. Where?

You reply from your subconscious. The need for physical to be so defined. The subtleness of spirit needing perhaps a shot in the arm. Our messages not as defined as you would expect in your state of existence. I wish you could hear me!

I am screaming for your attention. You almost see, then not. A new approach must be tried.

Do you not feel me? I stroke your hair in hopes that the vibration will transcend to a place where the molecules feel some sort of sensual feeling.

The frustration making the decision to proceed agreed to.

Do you hear me?

I await.

I continue to try.

I await.

I will never give up.

****

62

I Opened Myself To The Experience

Dear Friend,

I took the last breath this day fixated on the gates of Heaven. The life lived a good one with no regrets upon my actions. It was a god fearing one where I thought I knew my place in the hierarchy of all things.

At first it was exactly as I expected, a flash of light, a tunnel with crystal celestial cast of who I knew and did not know. It was all progressing nicely right up to the pearly gates. The satisfaction of knowing that heaven was just beyond them. It was not until I saw the curtain off to the side or was it more like a ripple in the fabric of my reality. I'm not sure. It reminded me of a movie I saw when I was a child. A mere man masquerading as a wizard in a place called Oz. It turned out to be a dream but the memory stopped me cold before venturing through the gates.

What if they were merely a fabrication set up to pacify a lesser evolved being while physical? What if behind the ripple was another being very much like myself providing the illusion of the pearly gates that I expected.

As the idea progressed through me the gates as I knew them dissolved before my eyes. I didn't know whether to be disappointed or elated.

The answer awaited me in the form of a beam of light that danced before me. Its appeal becoming clearer I saw it contained many facets of myself. It was revealed that I deserved a review and it could be attained. Not being sure what that meant I did not know how to reply.

After a few moments of thought I opened myself to the experience.

"Hey! Why not?" I thought.

The surroundings blended into my life I had just left. It was an ending reel of drama and action performed by yours truly. There were moments I remembered well and those that shocked me in the moment. It was indeed all there including the forgotten and denied.

It was quite a life if I do say so myself.

I looked about me expecting something to happen but nothing did.

"What now?" I thought.

What now indeed.

The pausing was confusing. I truly did not know what to do. I felt suspended with no support. Who was in charge here anyway?

"You are!" came the whisper.

"I am?" I replied.

"Well, what about those Gates? And where is St. Peter? On a break?"

"You are in charge," there it was again. I was beginning to become disturbed by the lack of what should have been there. By the way, were was God? I thought he was always with me?

"Look inside" came the whisper.

Where?"

"Look inside." There it was again. By now the frustration and disappointment had created quite a bit of chaos inside of me. Here I was dead and nothing was as it should be. No one had prepared me for this.

No one.

I sat cross legged on what I thought was the ground. I had come to suspect it might be the ceiling. That's how upside down my reality had become.

I waited.

and waited.....

and waited.....

and waited.....

By this time fully engaged in anger I shook my fist at this so called God who appeared to have forsaken me. Fooled by a false god, obviously created out of someone's imagination. I asked the surrounding again to fulfill my question.

"Where was God?"

Again came the whisper.

"Look inside."

Fully outraged I demanded to know where inside was. What was the inside? Was this just a cruel joke? Surely an answer at the very least could be provided.

“Look inside what?” I screamed.

At that moment a small beam of light showed up on the wall.

“Well, it’s about time” I declared standing facing in its direction. At last I was being given a clue. I desperately needed to know where to look. The light became brighter, a visual developing like a photograph.

“Look inside” came the whisper.

I closed my eyes falling surprisingly inside myself. The grandness of my spirit in that instant, of course I wanted an audience with God. I could only really find him inside….. me.

Once I embraced the god energy in me the rest was easy. I became the being I had only worshipped from afar.

****

63

I Was Only 27 Years Old

Dear Friend,

Today was just another day when I awoke this morning. Jumping up I stumbled into the kitchen to make coffee. Usually the preparation occurred the evening before. A new coffee maker with a timer forever changed my patterns of coffee drinking. However on this day I had forgotten to prepare. No matter. The whirl of the grinder jolted me more awake. It was 6:30 am and that gave me exactly one hour to shower, shave and make it to the train station by 7:30 am for a train into the city. It was like every work day predictable with obvious conclusions.

My job did not excite me so much but it paid well. I was a financial advisor for a major corporation known as Linco. It was the obvious career step after a brief internship right after college. It wasn't what I thought of as a child but it kept me in a comfortable life style.

There had been a few women in my life but none that prompted me to make that big step into marriage territory. Keeping my options open was more my style. I was only 27 years old….. plenty of time.

It looked like the beginning of a beautiful day when I stepped off my porch. Thoughts of the upcoming weekend filled my head.

A scrimmage Saturday morning, racquet ball in the afternoon with Peter, followed by poker, pizza and beer. Saturday night. On Sunday there would be the weekly dodging of my mother. Her pursuit of my spiritual path her main focus. She always invited me to church with her on Sunday mornings. Feeling some what guilty I would dodge her the best I could. One out of every six or seven weeks she'd tag me and I'd get stuck going. A total waste of time if you asked me but it made her happy.

Anyways my mind was thoroughly occupied this day on my weekend and the work day ahead of me. As if by remote I made my way to the train station. My mind a million miles away when the car hit me.

The most difficult part was the surprise of the impact. I felt my spine snap in two places. Funny how you can observe something like this almost in third person. It was like watching and being in a video at the same time. I should have been scared but I wasn't. IT should have hurt more but it didn't. My breath was difficult to catch but eventually I did. There was a lot of hub bub around me but I felt rather unnoticed. Apparently another guy had been hit as well. Looked like he was in worse shape. The paramedics practically ignored me to get to him. It was okay though. I was allright. Missing the train was irritating but there was another in twenty minutes. I'd just be late for work. No big deal.

Deciding to go back home to call work I made my way down the street. It was odd that no one seemed to be around the neighborhood. Guess everyone was down looking at the accident. Wonder if anyone noticed I had left. My back felt okay. Damn! What a morning. Nothing was turning out as I planned.

I ran up the steps to my place to hear the phone ringing. Picking up on the last ring my mother's voice came through loud and clear with her invitation to go to church with her on Sunday. My head was beginning to throb a little. Most likely because it was one of those weekends where I was caught by mother as she manipulated me into going to church with her.

Damn.

I agreed to meet her and hung up. I then dialed work but got a busy signal.

That was odd, there was a switch board there. It never was busy. I kept trying with no luck. Actually nothing seemed to work in my home. The phone rang a few times and oddly one of them was my mother, asking me to go to church again. She must be getting senile or something.

So I set out again for work. They were still cleaning up the accident. Poor guy got pretty messed up I guess. People were talking amongst themselves what a shame it was. They said his mother took it pretty bad. They said she kept screaming his name over and over. Odd. He had my name. They said she kept asking him to wake up and meet her at church. She said he promised to meet her there on Sunday. I turned my head to see my mother standing at the curb with her head in her hands.

The scene dissolved into church where I could see her sitting at the end of the pew all by herself.

Damn. It is Sunday already?

Making my way to her I notice the coffin. The priest is sprinkling holy water over someone.

Who had died?

I peered over the edge to see myself. My heart stopped and then I knew.

Now I look forward to Sunday church with my mother. I never miss. It's our quiet time together. An opportunity to blend with her and my guides.

****

64

Why Am I Still Aware?

Dear Friend,

Frozen in fear I was unable to realign the projected manifestation of my passing. To alleviate your fears I will tell you that there was no discomfort as defined in physical. It was merely a repetitive motion that became clear to my thoughts as I repeated scenarios. It was fortunate that other options had validity for me as the repetitive motion could have gone on indefinitely.

The opportunity of clarity provided by my questioning of the universe, which was frowned upon by those I participated with, was a distinct factor.

The stories told to me where reminiscent of fairy tales masquerading as the truth held me up in the transition between lives.

I'm not sure of the reasoning behind the misconception but from my current viewpoint the truth supersedes everything else. My evolution is my personal experience within my entity, any fabrication is insulting.

In this most previous existence the spiritual beliefs presented were a watered down version of the true intention. It would have made a difference to know the truth. It would have impacted my choice making to hear the true meaning of my existence. I was an intelligent individual who would have benefited from the concept of thought creates reality. Instead the presentation of a fear based reality prevailed upon my experience. I would have chosen differently given the power to do so.

So I write this brief dissertation as a corner stone for my next incarnation. I firmly believe in the pebble in the lake theory. Hopefully the ripples will extend to my next manifestation through this linear passage. All existence impacts itself through the linear. My truest hope is that this letter will cross my path futuristically and alter my perceptions. It might be the trigger to my understanding.

My only regret this time…..

….. No trigger.

****

65

I Wanted You To Know

Dear Friend,

I waited you know.

I waited, clinging to the tattered threads of a physical body long over due to retire.

It wasn't easy.

Although you perceived my awareness limited to the unfortunate state of a vegetable, I was indeed completely aware.

I just couldn't connect with the correct mechanics to make my body work. Simple tasks like moving my fingers and toes became monumental endeavors that were impossible to perform. My jaw was so tight that opening my mouth would have required a crowbar. I laughed internally at the ridiculous place I had ended up in. I always feared losing my mind in old age, instead I had lost control of my body. I don't really know now which would have been worse. It was a debate within that did occupy me for quite awhile as I lay there inert. Thank god, because without the dilemma I might have lost my mind as well.

I want you to know this.

I felt every stroke of your hand as it brushed my temple. It soothed the uncomfortable state reminding me of the way my own mother brushed my brow when I was a child.

It was so much so that I had to remind myself that it was you my daughter and not my mother. Interesting how life intersects and blends if one takes the time to examine it.

In the final days I learned to float up from my body which relieved some of my frustration. As I looked upon that poor old body I didn't think it even looked like me anymore. I guess that was when I lost my attachment to it. It was my soul that made that body who it was. It was a great revelation, believe me.

I wanted for all of you to be there. It takes time to round up eight children from across the country. I, of all people, knew that. It had been at least ten years since I got all of you together in one room.

I lifted out of that body to embrace each of you as the thoughts in your head reconnect with our past interactions. Some of them happy, some not as much. Be comfortable with the memory of our experiences for eventually we will meet again to reminice. We won't meet in heaven but a place of our own creation.

I wanted you to know.

So that all of you could wish me safe passage to the next phase. After being trapped for so long I was anticipating a new adventure. I can already see the probabilities moving towards me.

Rejoice.

I continue.

We will meet again.

****

66

The Mind Remains Focused

Dear Friend,

So attached to the body I feel my panic as it ceases its function. Where am I to go when it is done? My belief system has never made allowances for the after life, if indeed there is one. Much easier is the path that does embrace the notion of something more. The concept serving my life through its ups and downs. The repose of death a final event from which nothing would manifest. Our eternal rest the prize at the end we lived until now, with abandon.

Now in these final moments as the warmth of energy leaves my hands and feels cold beyond imagination I feel just as alive in my mind. Fear grips me again while wondering what will occur. Having long ago lost the ability to speak, the dialogue with myself overpowers my awareness as I step farther into the passage of death.

Despite all the failings of this body the mind remains focused. It feels like my consciousness is lifting out of this disabled frame, only to slip back when the realization of it hit me. I can feel the warmth leaving me. Why am I still aware? The darkness that was expected to shroud my existence has not occurred as expected. Instead as I lift up the light becomes brighter. My focus sharpening as the body is discarded. Surely this bodes of an un natural occurrence that will soon leave me in the nothingness I expected.

Looking towards the light I become acutely aware of others. What is this phenomena that holds me in its clutches. Everything I believed in, the annihilation and despair are no where to be found in this environment.

The foolishness of those who believed in such things ramble though my thoughts. Is this a final jab at my inability to accept their ideals and beliefs? If so, I wish the masquerade to cease so as to leave me in place.

I feel a hum, or rather a rhythm from deep inside.

What is it?

The light grows brighter with the images becoming more defined. I feel the final thrust of energy as the body is discarded. The features of the face not like me at all. Perhaps then it was my energy that gave myself its identity and not the physical features.

I wonder what the goal of this experience would be. Certainly its my consciousness reliving a moment before the final curtain.

I find myself curious as to where the light is coming from. Surely there is not a pinpoint or core from which it garners energy. Could it be a god of some sort conjured up by my inability to release myself as planned?

The light brighter still I encounter another whose definition is blurred within the reality.

Who are you? I ask.

Receiving no response I begin to feel the energy which is over powering. It does not attack but embraces me. My heart, although at this point I should not have one, fills with warmth.

"Who are you?" I repeat.

Still no response however the place from which I perceive all this becomes more defined. Shapes begin forming with in my thoughts bringing with it a clarity not embraced before.

Where is the light coming from? I ask to whoever or whatever may be listening.

The edges ripple but no reply is forth coming. My mind searches for the stability of the body while realizing that it was never truly needed.

How could that be?

My belief system regarded that body as the final enactment of this self, myself. Truly there is misconception here.

The light ever brighter I being to identify those I have known while living. Their features now more distinct I feel surprised at their presence. Is this a self delusion enacted out of my intense fear at finality? It would be much easier to dismiss their faces. However I find I cannot nor in these moments have any desire to do so.

The light now encompassing I ask again where does the light come from.

A small woman moves towards me. In a quiet moment I realize who she is….. my grandmother. She had no belief in an afterlife either. What was she doing here?

"The light is coming from you" she replied.

The idea of eternal existence extended its hand in the form of my grandmother. Its embrace settling the age old debate within.

I now move through thoughts to another state of existence. No longer in darkness….. but in the light.

****

67

It's All True

Dear Friend,

Outside the body I am free. The pulse of trauma that accentuates my current existence too much to bear.

Instead of replying to the anxiousness associated with the pulse, my consciousness has chosen to retreat to observe from a distance.

I see your commitment to my body that lays inert upon a crisp white sheet. A myriad of machines keeping track of the faulty rhythm now produced by a dying heart.

The clasp of your hand feels desperate. Know that the way has already been decided. There is nothing your energy can do to dissuade it. I am not afraid, the lingering opportunity for you to become adjusted to the moment of departure.

Your voice like a melody floats past. It's then I realize your viewpoint. I understand it because we had discussed it many times. Separation created by proposed death of one, ultimately causing great discomfort for the one left behind to carry on.

Realizing this I attempt to help you feel what I feel….. continuation at a higher vibration.

It's all true.

Your resignation with the projected loneliness not necessary. The end of our relationship defined only by a change of vibration. There is not a terminal energy attached here, only a significant readjustment. We are still solid in our love for you.

Outside of the body the possibilities surround us. Be patient. My feelings will never change for you, nor will I ever forget.

I have already created a portal through this hand that did not exist a moment ago. My thoughts of communication allowing the connection.

Outside the body we are free.

****

68

Your Time Will Present Itself And I Will Be Waiting

Dear Friend,

I know full well how much you miss my presence. The touch of your flesh accompanied by your eyes in mine, a loss that's difficult to get over.

Know that I am able to perceive all of the daily actions participated by yourself. Though you cannot feel the touch of my hand I still connect. It is important that you understand that I thrive, only in a different manner.

Crossing the distance between physical and spiritual not all that uncomfortable. In fact the event expanding what I considered to be me. A breath released causing the finality of the body actually an easy moment. It was not the moment of panic I had always feared.

If I could I would wipe your tears gently instead of watching you wipe your own in sorrow. I am not gone from you. The relationship continues. Attempt to believe in that old physical chemistry we shared, as it moves on.

Yes we will have to be patient while our energies realign to accommodate the new situation.

We can bemoan the perceived reparation or we can readjust while awaiting the final eternal reunion.

Close your eyes while reliving our physical closeness. The mind is a powerful reenactment device that could quiet and relieve the desperate longing.

Remember our moments, even the difficult ones as they all contribute to the energy between us.

Enjoy the rest of this physical, do the things we spoke of; with full knowledge that I am indeed at your side. How could I be anywhere else? Smiling I extend myself to your embrace, all you have to do is believe.

Create exactly what you want in full harmony with what we were, or should I say what we are.

Your time will present itself and I will be waiting. Bring with you all the memories. We will have much to speak of. Our blending the final reunion as we become one eternally.

With a smile I remember the impatience of your self that I know so well. It exists even in this moment trickling over to my space of existence. Be still while living your life in search of those connecting moments. They are there if you are observant.

It'll be the first feeling you have.

****

[Note: I hesitate to interrupt the flow of these messages with a personal comment. However since it is so very rare, note that out of all the thousands of writings that we have received over the decades from all manner of nonphysical beings including all the way up to Causal Plane and Source Entities and Guides, the message above is the first and only time that any nonphysical writer has ever used a semicolon (;). ~ Allen]

69

The End Is Just A Formality Of Flesh That I Bought Into

Dear Friend,

The wave of nausea crescendos within my stomach. My hands clench while preparing for the next one which is inevitable. I scoff at the idea that this assault is for my benefit. Defeat roars towards me like a raging fire. I wish to cover my eyes and ears while waiting for the final blow. Pain lingers in my extremities watching for opportunity to torture.

Some say that disease is the product of one's actions. The idea of that concept angers me deeply. Truly my life was lived better than this accumulation of misdeeds not deserving of this sentence.

I'm angry.

I'm afraid.

I dream of nothing as I face the end. My religion has abandoned me in my misery. The suffering all too much and not worth it.

They have sent me home. These doctors of medicine with nothing more to give have decided to stop. I don't blame them. Another dose of therapy would kill me for sure. The despair in my eyes reflects into theirs as they sign me out with relief. It must be disheartening for them as well. I mourn my health which will never return to normal. I mourn my faith in God which has been altered as well during this ordeal. If he truly existed this affliction surely would have been lifted from me.

So as I lay upon my sofa the energy of defeat surrounds me. I wish it would hurry along this cancer. Chewing me up in its path to my destruction. They said a bit longer, the definition of a bit eluding me.

Why not now!?

Why the wait.

The nausea returns as predicted. They said it would dissipate soon. Again another word left to my imagination.

Soon?

I reach for a wet cloth as the beads of perspiration roll down my neck. Where's the nurse they sent along to watch me? Escaped to the back porch no doubt. I would not want to be here either. I remember the morphine prescription deciding that the time is indeed ripe for relief. They said not to use it until I felt I had to. Well I feel the need vividly.

The nurse returns feigning concern as I beg for the relief of the drug. It flows into my arm numbing the pain somewhat. Wanting to be alone I ask for privacy. The nurse squeezes my hand before leaving announcing that she would be just outside.

I close my eyes hoping for a dream to release me from this moment. Drifting off to sleep the room dissolves into darkness. All I want is a moment of calm.

Just one.

At least sleep comes upon me, the hope for a dream still with me. The mist in my mind recedes revealing the framework of an alternate existence. One where the ravages of disease cannot overtake me. The drugs must be working for the nausea has disappeared. My extremities are mobile as I sit up from the sofa.

Since dreams are part of us then I should be able to do what I desire. To have a moment of peace is all I can focus on.

The surroundings blend into my childhood home. The smell of chocolate reaches my nostrils. It has been a long time since I was able to hold food down let alone chocolate. I wonder why the nurse is cooking chocolate. As I stand the feeling of buoyancy fills my body. Why did I not start the morphine sooner? I can actually walk with out interruption.

The kitchen looms ahead of me. With it the idea of having some lunch. I remember my mother's beef stew wishing she were still alive to make it. In the doorway I see movement. It looks like my mother in the kitchen of my youth.

"Sit yourself down. I am almost ready." She says.

Instinctually I wash my hands before sitting down. I wonder where the nurse is but suddenly lose interest. My mom has set a huge bowl of beef stew before me. I'm not nauseous but surprisingly hungry.

"Eat up" she urges.

"I have chocolate cake for dessert."

The sound of her voice leaves me feeling much better than I have in a long time. The despair leaves me slowly hovering however just outside of my eyeline. What has occurred I wonder? The answer eludes me as I start on the cake.

I do not want to awaken from this dream. It's been so long since there has been relief that I cannot bear to wake up. The chocolate distracts me as my mom reaches towards me.

"You don't have to wake up" she says.

I laugh to my self that she still is in her own little world. Oblivious to the outside world she existed solely in her own creation.

"It's true, you know," her mouth forming the words.

"Go take a look at the couch if you don't believe me."

Confused, I walk back to the living room which is filled with hospice equipment. There I lie upon the sofa still as can be.

"What is this farce?" I think out loud.

The mirror image of myself disturbing the moment frozen in my thoughts. I feel determined not to return to that body. The despairing thoughts leaving me. I rejoice for what has occurred. It's over. The why of it all eluding me. The negativity still a concern. I walk back to the kitchen for more chocolate cake. My anger moves away, the fear non existent. The surprise of a future here with my mother astounding. My life was lived better than I thought, the end just a formality of flesh that I bought into. It recedes now to that life, its lessons though, transcending to here.

I am home.

****

70

Should I Go Back I Wonder?

Dear Friend,

The destruction surrounds me while I lay exhausted in my own sweat. The climate feels alternately hot and cold. No stability awaits at the end of each seizure. They tell me they will continue, getting worse each day. The idea plagues me having already considered that the worst was here.

So tired.

The sheets drenched by my exertion to control my body. Surely the clenching will help I think, knowing the falsehood of my hope. What am I to do? The end so distant in my perception.

Why must I endure this?

Another tremor ravages my arms.

What did they say?

Oh yes. The tumor grows. It pushes against the nerves leading through my skull, through the neck.

Inoperable.

That's what they said. The word malignant also came into play. The words of doom encompass my energy and I feel defeated. No hope is no hope. Why the charade of healing. Just give me something to send me off into oblivion with no fanfare. This body no longer viable for any sort of life.

Tremors again.

The headache returns to torture what remaining moments are left.

Unfair.

Unfair.

If I were still able I would pull their tubes from me. They feed a life that barely limps along.

Another tremor, my head pulses so hard. I try to stop it but to no avail. The doctors prescribe more pain medications to stop the headache but it does not ease the shaking.

My eyes close. The time of day meaningless as the chemicals subdue my alertness. A moment of calm. I see the lights dim through my eyelids. It must be night. I listen to my breath go in and out. It's rhythm lulling a sense of slumber. What good will it do for me.

None.

I simply wait for the end. Will it ever arrive.

I feel another tremor starting deep within, only this time it come from my heart area.

What does this mean?

It moves through me slowly quite unlike the others. Could it be the moment? Am I passing over?

I lift up out of the body by merely sitting up. The only thing holding me down is my disbelief. That's suddenly quite clear to me.

The pain still present but now beside instead of inside. The process in my mind wants to deny the experience.

I see myself.

How can that be me? if I am here? Confusion reigns but I push through the maze.

Where is the heaven so popular?

Becoming more acclimated I begin to look in other directions. The pain in my head has subsided, the tremors non existent. However when I see myself inert upon the hospital bed it still quivers. Should I go back I wonder?

Detachment fills me as I realize that it is not really me. The "me" is here moving towards a brighter focus. I choose to move on. The acceleration leads me to the light. A cliché would have left me furious before. Now soothes the heart as I move on.

No more tremors.

No regrets.

Thankfulness for the transition. I do not know what awaits but the path will be better than where I was.

I feel the darkness leave my thoughts. Each moment becoming easier shedding the pain and tremors a relief.

I move on with gratitude.

****

71

"What Will It Be Like?" A Question Asked By Every Physical Being At Some Point.

Dear Friend,

The pain settles behind my eyes this day. It has traveled extensively throughout my body. Some destinations have been more acute than others. Some have been muted chemically for relief. Mostly it moves on to another place. I have come to expect its arrival. Ironically my body would miss it as the adjustments seem more automatic these days.

My appreciation of a moment that reminds me of a time when pain was not me is filling me now. There is great effort involved in holding a writing instrument. Yesterday remembering how to spell my name was an effort.

Today is different. There is a presence around that holds me in its grasp. A long ago story of guardian angels clmes to mind. Though it feels different than I expected. No doubt that Sister Thomas Marie from the third grade would be pleased. Thinking of her now surprises me. I haven't given religion much thought for many years. Now here on my death bed it comes back into focus. I know I'm not searching for redemption. My life was lived as truthfully as I could make it. I suppose now that I am at the door curiosity would best describe it.

Combining the presence with my curiosity leaves no alternative but going for it. Something I pushed from my focus in hopes it would never materialize.

"What will it be like?" A question asked by every physical being at some point. Will it be what I thought or what I hoped for. Will someone I loved be there to meet me? Or when the light fades and my perception of physical is no more, am I the I in my head, just to disappear never to return?

At the beginning of the process in my instance I feel this presence. I know today will be the day. Mourning for the moon I will not see this evening I decide to touch all the things that had meaning to me in this life, of course physically it would not be possible. However, in the corridors of my mind they all wait in thought for my arrival.

I step forward. My memory of my first dog. Brewster running towards me comes into focus. I can feel his tongue brushing my hand as I give him a treat. The moment so real I can smell his breath as he jumps into my arms.

I turn my head into another focus. I see my brother getting ready to throw me a baseball. His hat pulled down over his eyes as he releases the ball. I know his true intent was to hit me in the head with it. His glee when I actually catch it. An afternoon with my brother a welcome moment since he's been gone for about 20 years. Yet right now as I run up to him I can see blood vessels in his temples pulsing. Somewhere I recall that he died of a stroke caused by those pulsating veins. Now it doesn't ring true as we walk arm in arm to our house in Iowa. It's all right here.

I inhale a moment and there is a remembrance of the pain. Should I take a pill? Maybe I won't need one if I go back to Iowa. There was not pain then.

It occurs to me that if I become lost in thought then there is no pain. A better path for sure.

So here it is my friend. Existence in the thought is the transition. Caught in the physical I step forward to spiritual. It's such an easy step. You will be met by whatever you can think of. The light of the next phase of existence is much brighter than the one you leave behind. It will be much better than you could hope for. It will be what you think.

I must go now. My thoughts are becoming more fulfilling. My focus much sharper. I am alive in my thoughts.

****

72

The Experience Continues

Dear Friend,

I never be learning letters the way my folks wanted. Always some thing getting in the way on my path to the school house. If it weren't the harvest, it was havin' babies. I recollect the letters but not the regular order one needed to be makin' words.

I had me a chalk board once but gave it up to a girl up the hollow who needed it. No. Letters were never my strength. My children reading me stories and replying to messages from kin off in Louisiana.

Till the day I died I never wrote on single note to anyone. So how could I be doing it now. The questions hang above me as I move the pen on the parchment.

The last moments under the quilt I helped sew with my mama were peaceful. I knew my time had come with no fear in my soul. The preacher had always told us that heaven was awaiting the righteous. The fear was not the death itself but the judgement of who was actually deserving of the gates of heaven.

I thought myself worthy but one never knows what they say is the will of god might be.

There was an intake of breath that seemed to catch in my throat on its way out. A cough came through that continued for longer than it should of. It left a rattle in my chest that echoed in my head. The sound grew louder and louder until I lost my viewpoint. I was no longer tucked snuggly in my bed I was born in. The quilt no longer about me.

So I waited to be shown the gates of heaven only to find there was no such thing. I saw my Mama standing in a doorway in the distance. She waved me to her though my mind knew that she been dead these last few years. I admit I was curious about what she was doing though the disappointment at not finding heaven surrounded me. Mama hugged me close, her scent of vanilla still clung to her after all these years.

"What are we doing here"? I asked.

"Time for you to remember" she replied.

Remember? Remember what? I thought I just passed through a good Christian life expecting to receive my reward in heaven only to find my mama in a doorway talking nonsense.

"You need to write to the others and tell them what you've seen," said Mama.

"But I can't write." I answered.

"Yes, you can. That's why you need to remember" said Mama.

She stepped out of the door frame revealing a swirl of experiences that I had indeed forgotten.

So I am writing, a remembrance of another life where I could. It's important to understand that the experience continues, the reward is not heaven. It's a sense of evolvement. The expansion of the mind while embracing all of it.

****

73

Cigarettes

Dear Friend,

The first time I smoked a cigarette was behind my father's garage when I was eight. A neighbor whose name now escapes me had procured a couple of half smoked butts from his parent's house for our encounter with what we saw as adulthood. A funny sense of superiority took over with a "ciggie" hanging on your lower lip. The other kids knelt in homage to two kids daring enough to do it.

I liked all of it. The prestige, the taste and yeah even the burning sear down your throat with that first puff. My body would shudder with rejection but my mind welcomed the hacking cough which I fought hard to control. It didn't take long to get used to the cough. It didn't take long to get a steady supply and it took even less time to become hooked.

By the time I was thirteen I was stealing whole packs from the market. Since I was doing almost a pack a day I had become very resourceful. I didn't take anything else, just cigarettes. After all it was wrong to steal, everyone knew that. I just needed to smoke that's all. At such a young age buying them was out of the question. Stealing them was the only answer. I felt bad about it and all but did it anyway.

During my teen years the need grew bigger. I was soon

smoking two to three packs a day. Quitting crossed my mind once or two times especially when a pretty girl refused to make out with me. More than once my mouth was compared to an ashtray. After that I tried to date girls who smoked also. It cut down on the bickering quite a bit.

All the cool people smoked. It was just a fact. The legend of my early partaking set me aside from those who were just starting out. I was considered a veteran. No one really tried to get me to quit. They just wanted to bum one off of me.

When you are young there is a feeling of invincibility that defines your actions. Thoughts of death never really translate in your daily life. The idea of "doing damage" shrugged off by the ability of young cells to regenerate.

No one really tells you what's coming when you get old. Well maybe someone did and I just wasn't listening. Taking it one step further I'll say I listened but I just didn't believe it.

I noticed that I had difficulty breathing now and then but hell, who doesn't. So smoking my way through my thirties the quantity increased up to 3 packs a day. It kept me thin, the nicotine replacing my need to stuff my face. Everyone said it wasn't healthy, but wasn't being fat healthy? No it wasn't.

Suddenly I turned forty, it wasn't as cool to smoke as it had been. New evidence came to light about what the smoke did to your lungs. My favorite movie star heroes were no longer puffing their way to fame. I felt abandoned by them, growing resentful as I lit up another.

Realizing my cool days were waning in the approach of middle age, I cut back to a pack a day. The lingering cough that had followed me through my forties did recede somewhat. I avoided the doctor for obvious reasons. Not needing the continued speech about the evils of smoking. No it just wasn't acceptable to light up anymore. The passing into my fifties confirmed all of that. It was then I went to the doctor because even with a few I had a great trouble breathing. I felt like an elephant was sitting on my chest most of the time.

For some reason the fear of suffocation filled me during a coughing episode. My doctor said my lungs were deteriorating due to all the smoking. Several times I went to the hospital to be "helped" with my breathing. It was a lousy price to pay for being cool as a kid. Just lousy.

All of this rambling brings me to the point of this piece, my death.

I recall the last day quite well. The ventilator was churning away giving some relief to the heaviness in my chest. It was a wonder I didn't have cancer….. so everyone said.

Breathing had now become the enemy with my desire for a cigarette ever present. Yes. I snuck one whenever I could. It helped me deal with the panic I would argue.

The last day of my life I was sitting in the window of my kitchen with my now ever present oxygen tank. As I looked out I could feel a tightness that seemed to increase with every breath. Suddenly my breath seemed to catch in my throat. It could not be inhaled. The panic swelled while I reached for a cigarette to calm me.

I did not want to die but I could not breathe. The smothered feeling came over me and I regretted ever smoking to being with. It was stupid to abuse myself that way but it was now too late.

I felt a hand on my shoulder as my panic began to ease. Turning around there was no one there but I felt it all the same. The breaths grew deeper allowing me to feel better than I could remember. So this is what it's like to breath normally.

I stood, walking away from all the equipment. It dawned on me that something was different. The hand on my shoulder taking me back to a healthier place and time. I didn't figure it would be this easy.

Next time around.

No smoking.

****

74

I Wish I Had Known This Before

Dear Friend,

My whole experience in this particular life was shaded by the church. Coming from a strict Catholic family of twelve children our whole home atmosphere revolved around its concepts.

I remember learning about God and as his children that we must adhere to his rules. Of course a place in heaven would be ours if we did. The opposite would be true, a place in hell if we didn't. The vivid stories of a martyr's suffering the torture of the stake was enough to bring us to our senses.

Suffering was a key word throughout the religion classes and sermons. My family never missed a Sunday mass, for if we did our lives were certain to go awry during the rest of the week.

I collected figurines depicting all the saints including Jesus and his mother Mary. As a child I was particularly enamored with a porcelain Mary that housed a hold water station. This way I was able to keep myself "holy" in the privacy of my own room.

I lived this regimented life path throughout, continually expecting a full reception of heaven upon death.

Along the way there were other beliefs that presented themselves but I knew God would want me to stay on the true path.

When I became ill in my early forties part of me felt an excitement at the prospect of seeing heaven. Naturally the other part was extremely reluctant to let go of living. I fought the disease of Lupus, a declining of my kidneys, for several years. Often in some of the more uncomfortable moments I thought of just letting go. I thought I became more spiritual in those moments, then the physical body kicked in with its desire to live so I didn't.

As the end grew nearer I prepared myself by attending more masses. The flow of the ceremony lifted me to a place of peace. In those moments I became ready to go. The final stages of the disease enhancing my way to heaven with the increased suffering.

It was an October evening when I went to bed for the last time. I never married so it was alone that I drifted off to sleep. I had had a difficult few days where the medicine and therapy just seemed to have no effect. I felt lousy, so sleep was a great way to escape it. I said my prayers hoping for relief.

I thought I was having a dream at first. The Mass had just begun when some annoying person kept nudging me during the Epistle. I kept shushing the idiot during the sermon. What was his problem? The night appeared full of Masses, one following the other until I was wishing to wake up.

It's odd when you feel a déjà vu. It's difficult to piece together what's real and what's just made up in your head. I have to say, there is great confusion before the truth is revealed. It seems that the Masses were not dreams after all, only attempts to wake me thus the annoying talker.

All of it, my linear was a self made delusion. Instead of a final resting place, I stand on a springboard for infinite creation.

I wish I had known this before.

****

75

The Phone Call Three Days Later Was A Shock To My System

Dear Friend,

I awaited death with a stoic attitude. After all at the age of seventy nine what could I expect my future to hold?

My body was slowly betraying me at every turn. Between my hardening arteries, arthritis and stomach problems I managed to squeeze in some cancer.

It started with a bang in my right breast. The doctors diagnosed it as aggressive so the full treatment was necessary. They cut off the breast ad blasted me with enough chemo to send it to hell and back. Now the breast I certainly didn't need. I said "take both of them off if you think it would help". The doctor merely smiled and said no, one would be enough.

I could feel the chemo eating me alive. With all my other ailments there was usually a moment to recover. In this case it was a relentless battle inside of me. The treatments were spaced apart by three weeks. As soon as I would feel better it was time to start again. I don't remember ever feeling worse.

The medical staff tried to make me as comfortable as they could but nothing they did really helped. So I put on a brave face and endured. There was a glimmer of hope when the "all clear" came after my follow up visit. The fear of dying was put to rest as I actually began to think about other things besides being sick.

My children of course had gathered when the initial cancer attacked me. They dispersed after all the chemo hoping I would continue to rally. I thought I would but deep inside I felt the clock ticking.

What do we really want? To live until one hundred years old? So in my mind there was preparation, but someone forgot to tell my heart.

I first notice the red mark while bathing. At first glance it resembled a small blister. It was red and inflamed, hurting like a bee sting. I assumed it was some sort of bug bite so I ignored it. In retrospect it was probably a stupid decision, well at least.

The decision to tell my doctor came when the red mark had spread to my under arm area. Sweating can be extremely painful when you have a huge blister. I think I was looking for a remedy, surely he had some antiseptic or the like to fix it. The idea never crossed my mind that it was skin cancer. Only sun bunnies get that. I had not been in the sun for years.

My doctor's eyes widened when he saw it. The scraping of cells needed for testing was extremely painful. I went home feeling bruised and sore to await the results. At that point I didn't feel the need to alert my family. After all it was probably the shingles or something. A medicated ointment was all the was needed I thought for sure.

The phone call three days later was a shock to my system. It had come back this cancer only this time on my skin.

"Well, cut it off!" I exclaimed. The unfortunate news was that it would most likely come back regardless of treatment. So that meant I was pretty much a goner, that much I could accept. It was the pain of the inflammation that was too much to bear and it was spreading.

Now what I haven't told you is a little of my history. I grew up in a loveless marriage. Both of my parents being not very demonstrative in displays of affection. It wasn't that they didn't love me, they just felt uncomfortable with hugging and touching. Consequently I too remained uncomfortable with it throughout my own life. My children often chastised for what they felt was an affliction. Their father often held them close which was something I hardly ever did. I tried to please them but deep inside it just wasn't comfortable. It didn't however diminish my love for them, no, not at all.

I waited to tell them as long as I could about the return of the cancer. It had become painful for my clothing to even touch it. Of course they asked me what was wrong. When I told them they all wanted to hold me. It was so painful I backed up revealing just how bad it was.

From then on it was all down hill. The oozing sores spread over my body like a plague. I started to wish it would just be over with. Why was I lingering in this now almost useless body. My skin felt like it was on fire. I looked terrible which turned me into a recluse because I was embarrassed to have anyone see me. Sitting as still as I could I hoped for a moment of peace. The pain medication they gave me turned my mind to mush so I had to choose between being a lunatic or pain free. Most days I chose to be a lunatic.

I wondered why life turned out this way. What did I do to deserve to suffer this way?

The moments with my children were now filled with longing to hold them or to have them hold me. Just the touch of their hands on me, though painful filled me with such warmth. I began to regret the lack of touch becoming depressed that I had wasted so many years.

It just wasn't fair.

It was in front of the television that I drifted off. One minute I was thinking about an additional pain pill….. the next I was outside that hideous shell of a body. The relief immense as I basked for the first time pain free.

Thoughts of why so much pain occupied my mind. I could see my children as they sat at the funeral.

The "why" so poignant but elusive. Then it hit me…..

It was all to learn the value of touch.

Of course.

It occurred to me that I had circled the issue more than once. I guess I had to create the lesson with a lot of punch, but you know what?

I get it.

****

ABOUT THE AUTHOR

The short version is that April Crawford is one of the world's most naturally adept Full Body Open Deep Trance Channels and Mediums. April is also a bestselling author, with many published books in print. You can find all of them in both print book and Kindle digital formats on AMAZON.

If you would like to schedule a telephone consultation/reading with VERONICA or learn more about April Crawford and VERONICA, The Free Newsletter, The Inner Whispers Interviews Podcasts, or any of their books:

www.AprilCrawford.com

PLEASE NOTE: The consultations/readings offered by April Crawford involve speaking directly with the nonphysical Causal Plane Entity and Guide that we named VERONICA. Any topics may be discussed. The sessions are two-way fully interactive and conversational in nature. However, direct conversations with specific loved ones or friends that have crossed over are not something offered to the general public. Those with the means to facilitate advanced research projects are welcome to contact us with their proposals in that regard.

Printed in Great Britain
by Amazon

70711483R00129